NEW DIRECTIONS FOR STUDENT SERVICES

John H. Schuh, *Wichita State University*
EDITOR-IN-CHIEF

Elizabeth J. Whitt, *University of Illinois, Chicago*
ASSOCIATE EDITOR

Serving Students at Metropolitan Universities: The Unique Opportunities and Challenges

Larry H. Dietz
University of Missouri-Kansas City

Vicky L. Triponey
Wichita State University

EDITORS

Number 79, Fall 1997

JOSSEY-BASS PUBLISHERS
San Francisco

SERVING STUDENTS AT METROPOLITAN UNIVERSITIES:
THE UNIQUE OPPORTUNITIES AND CHALLENGES
Larry H. Dietz, Vicky L. Triponey (eds.)
New Directions for Student Services, no. 79
John H. Schuh, Editor-in-Chief
Elizabeth J. Whitt, Associate Editor

ISSN 0164-7970   ISBN 0-7879-9882-6

NEW DIRECTIONS FOR STUDENT SERVICES is part of The Jossey-Bass Higher and Adult Education Series and is published quarterly by Jossey-Bass Inc., Publishers, 350 Sansome Street, San Francisco, California 94104-1342. Periodicals postage paid at San Francisco, California, and at additional mailing offices. POSTMASTER: Send address changes to New Directions for Student Services, Jossey-Bass Inc., Publishers, 350 Sansome Street, San Francisco, California 94104-1342.

New Directions for Student Services® is indexed in College Student Personnel Abstracts and Contents Pages in Education.

SUBSCRIPTIONS cost $54.00 for individuals and $90.00 for institutions, agencies, and libraries. See Ordering Information page at end of book.

EDITORIAL CORRESPONDENCE should be sent to the Editor-in-Chief, John H. Schuh, Campus Box 8, Wichita State University, Wichita, Kansas 67260-0008.

Cover photograph by Wernher Krutein/PHOTOVAULT © 1990.

Jossey-Bass Web address: http://www.josseybass.com

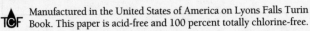

Manufactured in the United States of America on Lyons Falls Turin Book. This paper is acid-free and 100 percent totally chlorine-free.

CONTENTS

EDITORS' NOTES

Among the distinctive characteristics of U.S. postsecondary education are access, choice, and variety. Students in this country have a diversity of choices as they seek college admission. Although much debate has occurred over whether the choices for access to higher education should be dependent on one's ability to pay, the variety provided by our institutions of higher education is still the envy of many countries of the world. Theoretically, one could begin a postsecondary experience in a trade or technical school, transfer to a program in the college degree track at a community college, enroll in a baccalaureate degree program at a public or private institution, and finish graduate or professional school in a proprietary, public or private institution. The size of these institutions could vary dramatically, from a few hundred students to more than sixty thousand. Also, a student could choose to attend an institution away from her primary residence in a rural setting and live on campus or off campus in a variety of options. Conversely, a student can decide to live at home with his parents or spouse in an urban or metropolitan setting and commute to classes.

The possibilities of choice boggle the mind, especially as college administrators contemplate how to meet the service needs of diverse student populations with differing needs, abilities, and aspirations. It becomes an even greater challenge when one realizes that most institutions are confronted with students who fit into not one but several of these "life situation" categories. Thus, the challenge becomes one of how an institution should plan, program, and budget to meet the diverse and changing demands for services and resources. This challenge is faced by student affairs administrators regardless of the type of institution, but it is particularly demanding in a metropolitan university setting. A paucity of research is available about students who choose to attend metropolitan universities, and little opportunity exists for sharing ideas and expertise on how to meet the needs of these less-than-traditional students.

There have been several attempts to understand the unique needs of students attending institutions other than the traditional, primarily residential colleges and universities located in relatively rural settings. At a conference in 1985, representatives from the National Association of Student Personnel Administrators (NASPA) Urban Affairs Task Force and the "Urban 13," a consortium of institutions from the National Association of State Universities and Land-Grant Colleges (NASULGC), met to discuss the mission of student affairs at urban institutions. A monograph, *Student Affairs Programs at Universities in Urban Settings,* was written by Jones and Damron (1985) to capture the discussions from the proceedings. This document was helpful in citing the definition of an urban institution taken from the Higher Education Amendments of 1980. However, the authors identified several criteria to help define an urban or metropolitan institution, including that it should be "located in an urban or metropolitan area with a population of 500,000 or more" (Jones and Damron, p. 6). This document also published the research findings from other authors who had studied various aspects of the topic. Perhaps the greatest contribution to emerge from this 1980 document, however, was the development of some of the benchmarks identified as essential services for those attending an urban or metropolitan institution. This was, perhaps, the first document devoted exclusively to the uniqueness of the student attending an urban or metropolitan institution from the perspective of the student affairs administrator. However, the document left much more to be explored.

The purpose of the present volume is to provide additional (and more current) insight for student affairs administrators at metropolitan universities. To limit the scope of this project, the focus is on serving students at *four*-year metropolitan institutions. Although *urban* and *metropolitan* are used interchangeably in the literature, for this publication we have chosen to use the term *metropolitan* since we believe it is more inclusive. Hence with the phrase *metropolitan universities* we include four-year urban and suburban colleges and universities that are not just located *in* their community but are also engaged in active partnership *with* that surrounding area. It is our hope that this volume will stimulate further discussions and research from our colleagues at community colleges and other metropolitan colleges and universities to enrich the body of literature and enable us to work more effectively in this challenging yet invigorating environment called the metropolitan university.

The chapters have been arranged to further define and address the topic of serving students at such universities. Chapter One, by Jeannette Seaberry and Joe Davis, provides a definition of the metropolitan university and a brief history, along with redefinition of the mission and defining characteristics that make metropolitan institutions similar. In Chapter Two, Richard Hoover examines the role and function of student affairs at a metropolitan university from a chief executive officer's perspective and offers advice for student affairs change agents on a metropolitan campus. In Chapter Three, Michael Ginsburg outlines common patterns and special challenges in the areas of organizational structures, budgeting procedures, and staffing; he encourages student affairs administrators to become actively engaged in institutional planning. Chapter Four, by Caryl Smith, Virginia Gauld, and LeVester Tubbs, with assistance from Richard Correnti, focuses on the challenges and opportunities related to campus life in an urban setting. In particular, the life situations of metropolitan students and the rich diversity they bring to the campus are explored for their impact on efforts to build community and enhance campus life. Chapter Five, by Richard Palm and J. Douglas Toma, addresses the unique opportunity and valuable incentives for metropolitan institutions to build community relationships and partnerships. In Chapter Six, Larry Moneta provides a brief look into the future of metropolitan universities, with an emphasis on new challenges and perhaps shifting priorities.

The editors wish to thank Jossey-Bass for devoting a volume to this topic; John Schuh and Elizabeth Whitt for having faith in us to produce the volume; our devoted and insightful authors, without whom we would have had limited knowledge to share; our staff, who contributed their expertise; our family and friends, who were patient with our overly ambitious workload; and our metropolitan students, who give us so many reasons to enjoy our role of serving students at metropolitan universities.

Larry H. Dietz
Vicky L. Triponey
Editors

References

Jones, J. D., and Damron, J. *Student Affairs Programs at Universities in Urban Settings.* Washington, D.C.: National Association of State Universities and Land Grant Colleges, 1985.

LARRY H. DIETZ is the associate vice-chancellor for student affairs and enrollment management and assistant professor in urban leadership and policy studies, School of Education, University of Missouri-Kansas City.

VICKY L. TRIPONEY is associate vice president for campus life and assistant professor in the College of Education at Wichita State University and currently serves as both a member of the national board of directors and the Region IV-West vice president for the National Association of Student Personnel Administrators (NASPA).

This chapter conceptualizes the scope, notes the historical roots, and highlights the focus and mission of the metropolitan university in its relationship to and impact upon the urban community.

The Metropolitan University: History, Mission, and Defining Characteristics

Jeannette Seaberry, Joe L. Davis

One role assumed by universities in American society has emerged consistently. That is, institutions of higher education have been expected to be forerunners as places for creating knowledge and addressing relevant, contemporary, societal issues. Universities in large cities are strategically situated to play this unique role of serving needs and expectations because more than 80 percent of the population will, by the year 2000, reside in urban areas (U.S. Census Bureau, 1991). These universities, sometimes called metropolitan universities or "multiversities," extend the focus on externally oriented activities to include more causes and occasions for a two-way flow of continuous interface, feedback, and adaptation of city intellectual and suburban satellite constituents (Kerr, 1983). Namely, metropolitan universities are destined by their mission to become the land-grant institutions of the twenty-first century.

This chapter covers the historical background (especially the impact of World War II) and the changes in community, technology, and society related to the metropolitan university's mission, goals, and partnerships. Understanding the historical movement, beginning with the German research model, moving to agricultural extension, progressing to the liberal arts model, and concluding with the present technology-driven outreach model helps to conceptualize the framework of the evolving metropolitan university.

Historical Background

The bedrock model of what we now call metropolitan universities dates back to the eighth and ninth centuries and incorporates many of the earlier conceptualizations attributed to institutions of higher education. The explicit task assigned

New Directions for Student Services, no. 79, Fall 1997 © Jossey-Bass Publishers to universities—promulgated by intellects from Aristotle through Wilhelm von Humboldt and Cardinal Newman to Thorstein Veblen, Abraham Flexner, and Robert Hutchins—was to be the prime resource for societal intellectual development (Lynton and Elman, 1987). Historically and strategically, universities have long been places embedded in (oftentimes as) the heart of population centers; hence they reflected the core issues, demands, and needs as well as the values, priorities, and aspirations of their surrounding society. References to early regional universities date back to Salerno in the ninth century and include famed institutions in Paris and Oxford established during the twelfth and thirteenth centuries; all were centrally located within great European cities. Although images of these institutions reflect self-containment and isolation, populated by students engaged in the pursuit of knowledge for its own sake (Lynton and Elman, 1987), scholars attending these early institutions of higher learning also were trained in the professions of language, law, philosophy, theology, and medicine to respond to the immediate needs of their society (Hathaway, Mulhollan, and White, 1990).

The emergence of what we now call metropolitan universities as commonplace on many local landscapes is in many ways a recycling to earlier times, when connections to the surrounding regions were paramount and included within the university mission. Observations by Bacon, Dewey, and Whitehead note the responsibility and tradition of American universities as being responsive to both situation and society. Replicating the historic model, metropolitan universities came to have responsive, constructive roles linking together campus, commerce, and community (Lynton, 1995). These modern universities are defined by mission, rationale, and relationship characterized by their collaboration with and contribution to the surrounding region. Ashby (1967) noted that these evolving universities, having the same boundaries as the state, would be principal centers for creating new knowledge and major mechanisms for application, extension, and dissemination of such information to constituents.

Historical Background in the Early United States. The developing model of the metropolitan university was only beginning to take root in the United States in the early 1800s. During antebellum times, separate new facilities for advanced learning began to appear that were different from the training and research traditions typically associated with universities and higher education. These differing types of institutions were committed to liberal arts education and teacher training. The popularity of the institutions was quickly recognized by the Congress in searching for answers to the call for assistance with domestic economic problems related to agriculture, engineering, and teaching. The attention of government resulted in the first Morrill Act (1862), which created land-grant universities in every state of the union. A major thrust of this legislation was to equalize opportunities for access to higher education. These institutions educated students for career entry, extension (that is, agricultural and mechanical education), and research activity. The second Morrill Act (1890) regulated federal appropriations to support the land-grant institutions, with the intent of making higher education available to women, working-class students, and residents in remote areas. However intended, this did not expand higher education opportunities to African Americans, as most states prohibited integrated schools. In response, states developed "separate but equal" facilities, thus beginning the development of black colleges in the United States.

The Hatch Act of 1887 further expanded the idea of reciprocity between higher education and community with explicit informational exchange related to agriculture. In 1914, the Smith-Lever Act provided federal resources for continued cooperative extension. Universities engaged in teaching emerging agricultural skills and in continuing education efforts to update the steady stream of new information for rapid diffusion and absorption into the economy and community. Knowledge, techniques, and research were recognized as essential to classroom content, as well as being available in the public domain. Rudolph (1962), a renowned British scholar, conceptualized the utilitarian differences of scholarship as "a means and measure of self-development" by the British, as "a means in itself" by the Germans, and as "an equipment for service" by the Americans (p. 356). Later, Scott (1984) detailed another utilitarian viewpoint, the quest for "knowledge-as-a-product" compared with "knowledge-as-a-process" (p. 55), as distinguishing perspectives between British and American universities respectively.

The nineteenth-century utilitarian approach of American universities combined the strong components of the research characteristics of the German system and the liberal arts approach popular in British universities. Andrew White, the first president of Cornell University, envisioned graduates of higher education as "pouring into the legislatures, staffing the newspapers, and penetrating the municipal and county boards of America. Corruption would come to an end; pure American ideals would prosper until one day they governed the entire world" (Veysey, 1965, p. 85). The goal of the American university in the decades following the Civil War centered on a liberal education, including values clarification and career development, that would extend the dissemination of knowledge widely and effectively to both collective and individual users, matching the vigorous, changing, and expanding society.

Historical Background Since World War II. After World War II, institutions of higher learning were categorized to highlight the contrast between the intellectual and academic focus of traditional institutions on the one hand and the interactive collaboration of other types of universities, ones that were more aligned to social constituents (Scott, 1984). As a result of this taxonomy, the metropolitan university continued evolving and expanding to fit the demands of its ever-changing, knowledge-based local constituency. Thus it acquired a broadened scope to accommodate a wide variety of intellectual activities and priorities. Clark (1983) and Norris, Delaney, and Billingsley (1990) write that universities could no longer concentrate on the initial creation of material knowledge; rather, the urban academy had to mobilize its resources to participate in transferring and disseminating technological advances to meet the needs of modern society. Lindblom and Cohen (1979) describe the role of higher education as providing usable knowledge to be applied to an actual problem or task. The metropolitan university was to be a place where knowledge could be aggregated and synthesized into multiple realities, with contradictions explored, critical reasoning applied, and factors interrelated. Incorporating students' clinical and practical experience from industry into the classroom setting resulted in an enriched curriculum, narrowing the gap between real and applied perspectives.

In this way, the reciprocity between practice and theory of the university and the surrounding community results in a logical, coherent model for the campus and community to merge the goals of new technological needs and advancement of knowledge. Baker (1983) succinctly labels this process of interface between the university and its external constituencies "organizing knowledge for action" (p. 110). Currently, the metropolitan university is in a phase of rediscovery and renewal using a fundamental concept rooted in land-grant institutions: combining research with active extension service.

Defining the Metropolitan University

Grobman's redefinition (1988) of the metropolitan university entails specifics of the constituencies served and specialized course offerings related to what would be obvious needs within the socioeconomic parameters of the metropolitan locale. Writing in the *Chronicle of Higher Education,* Thomas Bonner depicts the metropolitan university as follows: "It is not merely a university located in a city; it is also of the city, with an obligation to serve the needs of the city's diverse citizenry. It has a special concern with issues of urban life. It does research and provides intellectual leadership. . . . It uses the city as a laboratory, clinic, and workshop. . . . It offers access to higher learning to people of all classes. . . . It listens to the community as a means of keeping in touch with its mission and its conscience" (Bonner, 1981, p. 48; cited in Grobman, 1988).

Rediscovering the Mission

Changes in society's expectations for higher education create a demand for a different type of institution and a very different institutional response to today's problems. Instantaneous communication in this technological age does not allow for contemplative responses, with their lengthy deliberation and even more time required for implementation outside the ivy-covered walls of the institution. Modern educational, business, and political leaders need and expect rapid response to the pressing issues and problems confronting them daily. Such immediacy does not mean the institutional response should be any less deliberative or contemplative, but the response delivery time must be shortened. Higher education administrators and faculty must share ideas and analyze problems with one another and develop consensus of opinion more efficiently in order to provide more timely response to the community. A course syllabus or a new program that takes a year to develop and two or more years for passage and approval by numerous institutional, systemic, and academic committees may well be outdated before it can be delivered to students.

Research. The community is a laboratory for the metropolitan university. Although basic research is an important component, the institution must develop its research agenda to meet the current and future needs of the community. Responses to these needs usually come from applied research studies as opposed to basic research. This merger of applied research and community is evident in the number of faculty at metropolitan universities who seek community-service or application grants to implement field studies. Community collaboration is extended and enhanced by these service grants, which provide interactive opportunities for faculty members from metropolitan universities and local education, business, and service leaders.

Both basic and applied research in collaboration with area businesses, schools, government, and social agencies are natural ventures that strengthen the partnership between the metropolitan university and the community. From these partnerships, benefits evolve for both the university and the agency. Students benefit from practical research experiences; universities receive contributions or royalties; and agencies get expert consultation, equipment, and new knowledge. Well-planned joint research ventures provide winning partnership for all parties, although these agreements must be well crafted to define ownership of copyrights, licenses, publication rights, and other resulting intellectual property.

Teaching. If the community is the research laboratory for the metropolitan university, the community populace is the student body of the metropolitan university. Davis, Kaiser, Hoover, and MacLean (1995) found that at urban institutions "students were characteristically older, attended part-time, scored lower on entrance tests, were employed, and tended to come from lower socioeconomic backgrounds" (p. 93). Lynton and Elman (1987) note many factors that are contributing to fundamental changes in the trend patterns found in higher education: "Instead of being full time and continuous, [enrollment] is becoming spread out, recurrent, and increasingly part time. Instead of being 'front loaded,' with learning preceding doing . . . higher education is becoming continuous and lifelong, with learning and doing interspersed" (p. 87). Students with varying work histories and significant life experiences demand different types of teaching approaches and learning environments. The traditional lecture method must be used sparingly, if at all. These students respond favorably to interactive teaching methods that resemble real-world situations. Case methods, collaborative teams, and projects with meaningful involvement work best. An inviting classroom climate also is necessary to actively engage these new students in the learning process. Foremost, unless students are treated with respect as adult learners they will seek knowledge from a more accommodating source. Given the increase in competition for students in higher education, the merger process of learning applied to doing cannot be ignored.

Faculty are seeking new modes of delivering educational material and experimenting with different time blocks to reach the student of today. Faculty have a responsibility to make sure these changes are pedagogically sound and technologically current. A review of institutional class schedules and promotional materials reveals a wide variety of class delivery, including the Internet, interactive television, weekend courses, courses given one evening per week, technologically advanced delivery methods, compacted learning, and credit for employment-related training. Innovative responses and changing constituencies have modulated teaching approaches and practices, yet much of the education process remains rooted in traditional values. For example, most institutions continue to specify fifteen contact hours per semester hour of credit, and they continue to require synthesis, integration, and application of course content over a specified time period, thus reinforcing a utilitarian concept that knowledge is a process over time. New methods of teaching and delivery must be used and evaluated in response to ever-changing technology, students, and knowledge base.

Service. The concept of "extension" has been superseded by terms such as *outreach, collaboration, partnerships, external orientation,* and *consultation* to describe the mutuality between the metropolitan university and the community. Faculty more often are proactive in establishing these ties; however, there are examples of community groups initiating programmatic changes at metropolitan institutions, including such new programs as black studies, Latino/Latina studies, Native American studies, and women's studies, and curricular changes such as information science and technology. Many times, after a need has been identified constituencies of metropolitan universities express disbelief at the time it takes for the institution to respond if the solution involves academic program development or course development. Metropolitan universities must be more timely in their response in this rapidly changing environment.

Faculty must expand their view of colleagues to include practitioners from the constituent groups served by the university. Faculty at metropolitan universities view service in a broader perspective than in the past. Components of service involve what the institutional faculty can contribute, but of equal or greater value is what the institution and faculty members gain from the service endeavor. Community-based service activities often are the beginning of long-term partnerships with reciprocal benefits for students, the institution, and the community.

Metropolitan institutions are forging cooperative agreements with businesses involving joint learning, teaching, and experiential opportunities, whereby some employees teach classes, and students interning within the business directly apply what they are learning. These joint ventures may share a common campus or space within the business. Nonprofit community agencies and governmental entities are also partners in this trend.

Defining Characteristics

Metropolitan universities are defined by a variety of characteristics that set them apart from the traditional Carnegie classification of institutions of higher education. The most noticeable difference is the vision that a metropolitan institution develops for itself. This vision leads to a specific mission statement

*As we move into the twenty-first century, the role of student affairs
at metropolitan institutions will continue to change as the role and
mission of the institutions change. Student affairs personnel must be
active in developing and providing services needed by students that
also help reinforce and support the learning community.*

The Role of Student Affairs at Metropolitan Universities

Richard E. Hoover

Historically, student affairs professionals have been charged with developing programs and services that respond to the needs of individual students as well as to the needs of the college or university. Thus, student affairs is one aspect of the institution that has experience with (1) being flexible in accommodating growth in both numbers and increasing heterogeneity of the student body, (2) being adaptive to the changing nature and structure of higher education, and (3) providing broadly for the perceived needs of the students and the institution. Whatever the future has in store for higher education, student affairs will continue to be responsive to changes in society and to the needs of individuals, just as has been true in the past (Shaffer, 1993).

As we move into the twenty-first century, the role of student affairs at metropolitan institutions will continue to change as the role and mission of the institutions change. Student affairs personnel must be active in developing and providing services needed by students that also help reinforce and support the learning community. Interpreting the institution to prospective students and to the metropolitan community is a vital role for student affairs. Finally, student affairs professionals must offer programs and activities that enable students to experience opportunities for leadership as well as those that develop mature appreciation and respect for others while pursuing social, cultural, artistic, spiritual, and recreational interests, in addition to their academic pursuits.

The author wishes to acknowledge the literature research contribution of Rita Henry, assistant to the vice-chancellor of student services and enrollment management, University of Nebraska at Omaha.

Failure to be accountable in our efforts to recruit and retain students could lead to the replacement of student affairs professionals with *other* personnel, offices, or programs that will attempt to meet the needs of the campus and students. Examples already exist in some institutions of companies being hired, on an outsourced basis, to recruit students; of traditional student services (including tutoring and other learning resources) being moved to academic affairs; of financial aid offices being moved to the business affairs area; and of registrar's offices being moved to academic affairs. However, when clearly designed enrollment management models are in place, the aforementioned activities remain within student affairs as interrelated units, at least in the most common organizational model. While continuing to react to changes, student affairs professionals must become full, proactive partners by assisting their institutions in determining their mission and primary purposes. Only then can these professionals interpret the institution to prospective students, parents, families, and other constituents. Whether an institution continues to exist depends a great deal on how well it demonstrates flexibility, adaptability, and responsiveness in meeting the needs of its society (Shaffer, 1993). This applies to student affairs units in higher education institutions as well as to the rest of the campus.

Delivery of Necessary Services

Student affairs professionals need to provide three basic services in contemporary metropolitan colleges or universities. It is not just *what* services are provided that is important, but also *how* they are provided that ensures continued viable student services. The three primary service areas are (1) recruitment of students, (2) retention of students, and (3) creation of a campus-life environment that is welcoming and allows students to feel connected to the institution.

Recruitment. Beeler and Moehl (1996) state that "Enrollments in public urban universities are particularly susceptible to demographic changes and market-driven local labor needs. Unfortunately, many institutions pay little attention to the manner in which students are recruited and supported, or the extent to which they are retained, until enrollments actually begin to decline" (p. 1). Student affairs professionals in urban, metropolitan areas understand that the age distribution of undergraduates attending is usually bimodal; they are traditional in age (seventeen to twenty-two) and nontraditional (older than twenty-two), creating two distinctly different student populations. However, most institutions struggle to understand the needs and expectations of their students. To further complicate the issue, myriad student subcultures exist within the age groupings; there are commuters as well as residential, inner-city and urban-suburban, economically advantaged and disadvantaged, minorities and international students. The differentiation becomes even more complex within a given group. For example, Rhatigan (1986, p. 6) encourages campuses with a significant number of commuter students to make even clearer differentiation within this group itself.

Once an institution has a better understanding of the students currently enrolled and the populations it seeks to serve, then plans can be developed to successfully recruit students from these service groups or areas. As the institution attempts to market its value to these populations, it is the student affairs professionals who must play a critical role. They coordinate and focus the various resources of the institution into educating the prospective students, their families, and support groups as to the value of attending the metropolitan university. "Many of the traditional-age students of the future will come from one-parent families where the only provider is the mother," John Schuh reports (1993, p. 52). He continues, describing these families as falling below the poverty line and as having non-college-educated parent(s); the student bodies of the future will have more students of color. "Campuses are already struggling with providing appropriate support to historically underrepresented students" (p. 53). As the numbers of such students increase, additional staff time, perhaps staff numbers, and additional program support may be required (Schuh, 1993).

Attracting first-generation, typically place-bound students to attend the metropolitan university is not an easy assignment. Student affairs professionals must be positioned within their institution so they can assist in determining the population it wishes to serve; they also must work closely with the academic sectors of the institution. Student affairs professionals must orient faculty about the message that should be delivered to the public about the strength of its academic programs and the linkage to cocurricular programs. Faculty are then able to assist in explaining the value of the educational opportunities being offered to their students. If faculty are helped to know their students better, they are more likely to adjust their teaching styles and personally assist students with learning. This partnership with academic colleagues assists student affairs professionals and the institution with effective personalized recruitment.

Developing partnerships between faculty and staff is essential to the recruitment and retention of students. It should not be assumed, however, that faculty understand the broader enrollment goals of the institution or the particular profile of the students in any specific academic unit. Profiles should be developed by the admissions office, describing the students targeted for recruitment. Once enrollment data have been gathered, another profile should be developed pertaining to those who have actually enrolled. The profile could include the average ACT/SAT scores of the entering first-year class; the percentage of men, women, ethnic minorities, foreign students on visas, and students with disabilities; the percentage of students receiving financial aid; and so on. More general information to add to the profile could include the percentage of transfer students, enrollment by academic unit and discipline within academic unit, percentage housed on campus, percentage belonging to fraternities and sororities, percentage working on campus and working generally (if the data are available), percentage participating in cocurricular activities, and the percentages in various age categories.

Further, the faculty should also know about student enrollment patterns. Metropolitan institutions tend to have a larger percentage of students who transfer and many who do not follow a continuous enrollment pattern. Students living in metropolitan areas may enroll sporadically, stopping out to devote more time to family, job changes, and other life circumstances, with every intention of returning at some point when enrolling in school fits as a higher priority. This fluctuating enrollment pattern of some students makes it incumbent upon the faculty and staff to be flexible and understanding of their situation so that the institution is perceived as a welcoming place to which they can return. Thus, faculty and staff are placed in a perpetual state of readiness to address the needs of students who may have to alter their academic plans and enrollment because of personal circumstances.

Faculty can also play a major role in student recruitment by seeking ways to collaborate with their colleagues at the elementary, secondary, and community-college levels. By offering to teach a class at other schools or conducting research with other such faculty, they can build bridges between institutions that result in positive relationships with colleagues, which in turn may lead to higher referral rates to each other's institutions. By virtue of their location, faculty at metropolitan universities have a unique opportunity to collaborate with the broader educational community, and in doing so help with their institution's recruiting effort locally.

Transfer students from community colleges often represent a large percentage of enrollment at metropolitan universities. Central to the successful movement of students from two-year community colleges to four-year institutions is a sound articulation agreement between institutions. Faculty can assist in this endeavor and must understand the importance of a smooth transition from the student's perspective. Articulation agreements must be reviewed annually and updated to include any changes. The document should then be distributed widely to academic advisors (on both ends), administrators, and key faculty.

Finally metropolitan institutions should host on-campus activities and events for prospective students and for faculty and advisors from secondary schools and community colleges. These may range from informal visits to sessions with faculty, academic competitions, or social events. The possibilities are endless, but faculty should be invited and integrated into the program.

Retention. Data collected through the Public Urban Universities Student Affairs Data Exchange (MacLean, 1996) demonstrate that attrition is typically quite high for undergraduates at urban and metropolitan institutions. Changing this high-attrition pattern has proven difficult, elusive, or costly. However, programs have been developed in many metropolitan institutions that demonstrate improved retention, but they usually are highly individualized, labor intensive, and supplemental to regular academic programs. Such efforts are not realistic when applied to the larger student body because of institutional budget constraints. One way of being able to offer individualized attention for selected student populations is to obtain grant funds such as the special program grants of percent in 1995. During the same period, higher education's share of total state appropriations went from 12.3 percent to 10.3 percent. It was during this period that public institutions imposed rapid tuition increases to make up for the decline in state appropriations [Pew Higher Education Roundtable, 1996, p. 2].

As we seek to forecast the future financing of higher education, we must realize that to the public-policy sector higher education is now primarily viewed as *individual gain.* The federal government apparently no longer sees higher education as a *public investment,* as evidenced by the major shift of federal financial aid from grants to loans. The government continues to be concerned with the accessibility of higher education, but that most commonly means increased debt for low-income students. State governments have many competing priorities, including health care, services for the elderly, social services, and the costs of the legal system and prison operation. As a result, the future appears to suggest constrained and limited public financing of higher education. Institutions have to clearly delineate their mission and purposes. In turn, student affairs professionals are limited to providing services and programs that directly and empirically support these goals; the value and impact of such services have to be measurable.

Assessment and Planning. At the present time, accrediting agencies are receiving increased attention to demonstrations of what they accomplish and how they accomplish it. With this increased scrutiny by the federal government, state governments, and professional organizations, accrediting agencies have been refocusing their standards and requirements. For example, recently the North Central (Accrediting) Association has inserted a standard that requires all higher education institutions to increase their objective assessment of the impact of educational programs. As a result, institutions are improving and increasing their modes of assessing learning. Student affairs programs appropriately are included in such evaluations.

In addition, as budgets become more constrained, administrators are being pushed into making decisions concerning what to offer students on more of a "cost-benefit" basis. As a result of increased requirements for assessment and cost-benefit analyses, student affairs professionals must move in this direction as well. To measure "client satisfaction" is one important form of assessment in the delivery of services. However, in the area of student development, quantifying the impact and value of programs and services becomes substantially more difficult. Regardless, whenever financial support or increased support is needed, then good data from substantive assessment are not only warranted but indispensable.

Assessment without a strategic planning process is shallow. After determining the mission and goals of the institution, student affairs professionals need to determine the goals for the services and operations of their division, delineate objectives, and assess effectiveness upon implementation. Although this process of planning and assessment cannot ensure continuation or guarantee additional funding, it contributes significantly to convincing those allocating funds and other resources that such services are viable and necessary.

Structure and Organization of Services. Historically, student services have been organized into departments that connote specialization. Since 1937, with the advent of the "student personnel point of view," much has been taught, written, and discussed about student development and the concept of educating the "whole" person. Yet from an administrative perspective, specialized offices have been created that "divide" a student's problems into pieces and require the individual to go from office to office to seek solutions.

In metropolitan institutions, students' time is limited, and they are impatient with standing in line for services or being shuffled to different places. Offices rarely have sufficient staff to manage peak loads because of budget constraints. Therefore, student services needs to move to what Coles calls "an eclectic, noncompartmentalized approach" (1990, p. 75). Where possible, student service offices that are related—for example, to broad categories such as enrollment management, student development, student life, and so on— should be consolidated or at least physically located close to each other. Then cross-training can be facilitated to allow for movement of staff at peak periods as well as assist students with problems that cross office boundaries. Another perspective would argue for the hiring of student affairs professionals who are versatile generalists so they can assist students who have complex or multiple needs. Examples already exist on many campuses of offices or centers responding to multiple needs of such special groups as African-American students, physically challenged students, and women returning to higher education.

How units are organized must also take into account the need to integrate these services with the academic mission of the institution. When we look at the three primary purposes for student affairs, (recruitment, retention, and campus life), it is critical to envision these areas with direct links to the colleges and academic departments in the university. Academic administrators and faculty should be asked to assist with recruitment planning and implementation. They can participate jointly with developmental programs in learning skills, tutorials, advising, and various other retention services. Faculty should have an integral role in various campus activities, as organizational advisors, volunteers with students for community service, etc., so that students have the opportunity to meet and get acquainted with faculty personally.

This does not negate the student personnel point of view and the need for student affairs to be organized for teamwork through a separate division. Rather, it recognizes the mandate to integrate student affairs into the learning community. To do otherwise raises questions of the relevance, value, and importance of student services.

This chapter began by suggesting that, historically, student affairs practitioners have been adaptive and creative as they worked for their institutions and their students. Student affairs staff work to serve the mission and goals of their institution; they strive to fulfill the needs of prospective as well as enrolled students; and they work to fully support the learning environment. Because of these factors, services offered must change as the clientele changes. Focused, planned, and highly productive student services that demonstrate their value will always have a place in environments that purport to educate the whole person. This is the vital role for student affairs in metropolitan institutions for as long as its professionals are looking to the future as change agents closely attuned to the diverse student subpopulations they serve.

References

Astin, A. W. *What Matters in College? Four Critical Years Revisited.* San Francisco: Jossey-Bass, 1993.

Beeler, K. J., and Moehl, P. J. "Continuous Improvement: A Way of Integrating Student Enrollment, Advising, and Retention Systems in a Metropolitan University." *Metropolitan Universities,* 1996, *6* (4), 17–33.

Borden, V.M.H., and Gentemann, K. "Campus Community and Student Priorities at a Metropolitan University." *Associations for Institutional Research,* 1993, Annual Forum Paper (ED 360 920).

Coles, A. S. "Student Services at Metropolitan Universities." *Metropolitan Universities,* 1990, *1* (2), 73–83.

Connell, C. W. "Information Age Challenge for Metropolitan Universities." *Metropolitan Universities,* 1995, *6* (1), 31–38.

Jacoby, B. "Adapting the Institution to Meet the Needs of Commuter Students." *Metropolitan Universities,* 1990, *1* (2), 61–71.

MacLean, L. S. "The Urban Student Affairs Data Exchange: Its Value and Uses." *Metropolitan Universities,* 1996, *6* (4), 9–16.

Murrell, P. H., and Davis, T. M. "Places of Community for Adults." *Metropolitan Universities,* 1990, *1* (2), 53–60.

Pascarella, E. T., and Terenzini, P. *How College Affects Students.* San Francisco: Jossey-Bass, 1991.

Pew Higher Education Roundtable. *Policy Perspectives.* Special Issue. 1996, *7* (1).

Rhatigan, J. J. "Developing a Campus Profile of Commuting Students." *NASPA Journal,* 1986, *24* (1), 4–10.

Schuh, J. H. "Fiscal Pressures on Higher Education and Student Affairs." *The Handbook of Student Affairs Administration.* San Francisco: Jossey-Bass, 1993.

Shaffer, R. H. "Whither Student Personnel Work from 1968 to 2018? A 1993 Retrospective." *NASPA Journal,* 1993, *30* (3), 162–168.

Wilmes, M. B., and Quade, S. L. "Perspectives on Programming for Commuters: Examples of Good Practice." *NASPA Journal,* 1986, *24* (1), 25–35.

RICHARD E. HOOVER is president of Hastings College in Hastings, Nebraska. Prior experience included fifteen years as vice-chancellor of educational and student services at the University of Nebraska at Omaha and ten years as assistant vice-chancellor of student affairs at the University of Missouri at Kansas City.

as a "perceived lesser brand," and consequently they must do more to convince the public to purchase their product. A decade ago, metropolitan institutions focused less on recruitment efforts, but the current trend is for increased staff to perform this function as marketing and sales techniques have grown more sophisticated and metropolitan institutions have attempted to retain their market share of eligible students. Recruitment efforts require more contact with students than is that case at other universities, which focus on one campus visit. At metropolitan institutions, recruitment efforts may include invitations for multiple campus visits and inviting prospective students to campus events.

Additionally, the staff hired to perform recruitment functions at metropolitan universities may differ in qualifications from those who perform this function at traditional institutions. Local experts who are well connected in the community, particularly those who can help with underrepresented minority groups, may be hired to assist with recruitment efforts despite their lack of job experience in the field of student recruitment. This approach results in a need for more staff training and development programs.

Diversity.   Metropolitan institutions generally have a higher percentage of minority students enrolled because larger numbers of minority individuals reside in urban areas. Because of internal and external forces, these institutions often must maintain an enrollment that closely mirrors or exceeds the minority percentages in the community. For these reasons, the institutions must recruit and retain staff who reflect the community composition so as to provide students with a variety of role models. A diverse faculty and staff is presumed to hold a higher level of understanding and sensitivity for minority student needs. Minority students often receive specialized support services provided by special student service units; this requires additional staff and financial commitments on behalf of the institution.

Athletics.   Given the urban character of the campuses, and the nature of student recruitment described in the admissions discussion earlier, most metropolitan institutions rely upon athletic programs that are reflective of the community and attractive to community members. Given the recent emphasis on basketball as the predominant participant sport in urban environments, it should not be surprising to learn that men's and women's basketball is the primary sport for most metropolitan institutions.

There is a clear difference between metropolitan university athletics and athletics at residential institutions. In metropolitan areas, there are many other competing interests for individuals who enjoy attending sporting events, including professional sports and those at other colleges. Rural campuses have little competition in this regard. As a result, athletics staff at metropolitan campuses must spend additional dollars on marketing and have less of a fan base for ticket sales, which affects availability and distribution of funds within the department.

Athletics at some metropolitan institutions may be less important, while at others it is emphasized. Comparisons among institutions can only be made when similarities exist in the level of competition (such as National Collegiate

Athletic Association, or NCAA, division membership classification), conference affiliation, and similarity of sports being offered. For example, institutions
with football teams competing at the Division I level within the NCAA have
significantly higher costs and staffing levels compared to a metropolitan institution without football that competes at a different athletic level within another
athletic conference. Major college football carries higher costs thanks to the
large number of athletes and coaches involved, in addition to higher administrative, travel, and recruitment costs.

Budgeting

Colleges and universities obtain their operating funds from a variety of sources
and then develop their own internal processes for allocating those funds. Both
of these processes require that institutional planning and organizational decision-
making systems be put in place. A system is needed to determine the appropriate
level of financial resources to support institutional goals, examine methods for
obtaining funds, and review the internal distribution of funds that are collected.

Each of these processes relies upon experts who have an understanding
of financial issues. Metropolitan institutions generally do not differ from other
institutions in their need to develop appropriate budgeting procedures.

Sources of Budgets. Institutional budgets typically consist of several different components: operating budgets, capital budgets, restricted budgets, auxiliary enterprise budgets, hospital operations budgets, service center budgets,
and unrestricted budgets. Student affairs units generally rely upon only a few
of these sources.

Operating budgets are derived from the primary source of income available to the institution. In public institutions, operating funds come from state-
allocated resources and tuition dollars. At private institutions, tuition dollars
serve as the main funding source for operating budgets. These funds generally
are earmarked to specific departments and programs. The institution may have
some control over internal allocation or reallocation of these funds.

Capital budgets consist of funds provided to the institution for facilities.
These funds may be utilized for construction of new facilities or maintenance
or renovation of existing facilities. Capital funds usually are provided to public
institutions by the state after a priority list is derived. Private institutions often
rely upon specific endowments or gifts to fund capital projects.

Restricted budgets consist of funds allocated to the institution by state, federal, or local agencies for specific purposes or from donations made to the institution by alumni or others who earmark the donation for a specific purpose.
Examples include such diverse issues as a federal research grant for laboratory
studies or a faculty chair in the English department. A restricted budget also may
consist of funds derived from student fees earmarked for certain expenditures.

Auxiliary enterprise funds are derived from student fees or generated income from the sales of merchandise or services provided by auxiliary operations. In some states, these funds may not be commingled with operating funds.

Hospital budgets are similar to auxiliary funds in that funds allocated for the operation of a hospital may not be reallocated for other purposes, and funds for other purposes cannot be redirected to the hospital. University hospitals commonly are found at metropolitan institutions.

Service center budgets usually consist of units whose budgets serve as a "pass-through" to provide a service for the institution. Essentially, all of the unit's operating funds are derived by charging other units for services. Examples of this approach include central word processing areas, telecommunications, and publications offices.

Unrestricted funds are generally very limited; however, an institution may have endowments that have been provided without any specific designation and that can be utilized at the institution's prerogative.

Many metropolitan universities also derive income from special user fees, in which students are charged for applications or transcripts, or for a differential cost of enrolling in certain courses or academic programs such as architecture, computer science, or engineering.

Student Affairs. Student affairs units typically receive the bulk of their funding from the operating budget of the institution. Those institutions funded by state or other public funds thus may find that mandates for the use of those funds have been imposed by state legislatures, the governor, and state higher education governing authorities. Funds may be specifically earmarked for one special type of program but cannot be reassigned without legislative authority.

Student fee revenue resulting from fees collected separately from tuition may support a portion of student affairs. Student fee levels are usually set in consultation with student committees who have some authority to review unit budgets and allocations to specific programs. Fee budgets at many metropolitan institutions tend to be higher than at traditional institutions for several reasons. First, student affairs divisions are not funded as well from institutional operating funds. Second, many metropolitan institutions are younger than traditional institutions, and hence the cost of adding services when a metropolitan institution was begun is higher than for a program started many years ago. Third, wages and construction costs are generally higher in metropolitan areas; thus, it costs more to provide services or build facilities.

Auxiliary enterprises are units that generate all or part of their operating budgets from sales or services. Units such as residence halls, bookstores, recreation centers, dining services, student unions, child care centers, and intercollegiate athletics are all examples of auxiliaries. Although auxiliary units generally are expected to be self-sustaining, they may receive some state or student fee funds, depending on state regulations, institutional policies, or institutional traditions. Metropolitan universities are more likely to house child care centers because this service is needed by students with children. Child care centers may be funded by a combination of institutional subsidies, student fees, and user fees. Institutions subsidizing child care centers are apt to do so in order to provide this service at a lower cost for students and support staff for whom the service would otherwise be unaffordable.

Another form of student affairs funding has been termed "fees for services." These fees are charged only to those students who directly utilize a service, distinct from student fees that essentially tax all students to provide a common good. Examples of the fee-for-service trend are fees for counseling visits or health center visits. Child care centers that are completely self-supporting would also be listed in this category.

Other sources of funds for student affairs units include grants for specific programs, income derived from rentals or leases of facilities to outside groups, bonds, capital funds, and earmarked funding provided by donors and corporations. Bonds are typically issued for the purpose of funding new facilities. Examples of bonded student affairs facilities are entertainment arenas, student unions, residence halls, and recreational or athletic facilities.

Budget Allocation Process. Once an institution obtains its resources, the funds are allocated within the institution through an internal process. Student affairs divisions typically receive small amounts, if any, of new resources when they become available, and often student service programs are viewed as easy targets during budget reductions (Pembroke, 1985). Academic programs and academic support services usually receive the top priority of key campus leaders. State legislators are more apt to accept the rationale for additional library funds or engineering college initiatives than to provide funds for student development activities. Thus, student affairs divisions usually receive fewer new resources allocated to the campus by the state. Additionally, when campus chief executive officers make internal reallocation decisions, academic programs typically are given greater priority.

Generally, the budgetary process utilized in colleges and universities varies among institutions. The budget process may be affected by a number of factors, including institutional character, participation, trust, openness of the process, centralization of authority, and demand for information (Meisinger and Dubeck, 1984).

Alternative Funding Sources. Given the lack of consistency in annual allocations for higher education at state institutions, and the instability of maintaining consistent enrollment levels at both private and public institutions, institutions have to locate other sources of funds. Vandament (1989) identified several other potential budget sources for universities, many of which directly benefit student affairs divisions: (1) increases in user fees, such as tuition and other fees, including innovative special fees that support hiring additional faculty, purchasing computers, or constructing new buildings; (2) revenue bonds to finance construction projects such as residence halls and entertainment arenas; (3) aggressive investment strategies; (4) income derived from increased enrollments resulting from enhanced marketing and recruitment efforts or new academic curricula that attract additional students to the institution; (5) private funds from aggressive development campaigns directed toward alumni or corporations; (6) joint financial agreements between the institution and industry for research or training; and (7) grants from federal or state agencies.

Budgeting Models. Budgeting has been described by various authors as the method utilized by the institution to distribute its resources or as a means of financial planning (Caruthers and Orwig, 1981; Lozier and Althouse, 1983; Wildavsky, 1984). The human dimension of "translating financial resources into human purposes" (Wildavsky, 1984) equates budgeting with other organizational processes. Many budgeting models have been or are currently being utilized by higher educational institutions.

Most budgeting is done incrementally. Changes in budgets from one year to the next are compared with the resources allocated during the previous year. This process results in very small changes since continuing commitments do not vary unless either new programs are added or significant budgetary reductions affect the unit. Political scientist Charles E. Lindblom described this concept as "the science of muddling through" (cited by Meisinger and Dubeck, 1984, p. 182).

Other approaches utilized by colleges and universities in the past include planning/programming and budgeting systems (PPBS), zero-based budgeting (ZBB), and formula budgeting. An emerging approach is termed *cost-center* or *responsibility-center budgeting.* Under this model, each "tub is on its own bottom" (Meisinger and Dubeck, 1984, p. 188) such that every unit is expected to either manage its prescribed allocation or become self-supporting by generating its own income. This model forces units to become more accountable for their own actions; however, it is also costly for each unit to hire its own financial expert.

Privatizing and Outsourcing. A current trend affecting student affairs divisions is the use of private vendors to provide services that were previously extended by the institution. Examples of this trend, which is often termed *privatization* or *outsourcing,* include contracting with firms to provide catering, management of facilities, bookstores, health insurance, psychological counseling, police and security, custodial services, temporary clerical staff, and project management. Each of these ideas has the potential to save a substantial sum of money expended by the institution to operate these units; also, the profits made by these firms can be shared with the institution in exchange for the privilege of the contract.

Outsourcing may have a negative effect upon the institution in several ways. University staff positions must be replaced by employees hired by the private vendor that is retained to perform the service. This practice may be controversial, particularly at campuses with strong employee unions. Another problem involves loss of direct control of the service until it is time for the contract to be renegotiated. Although the contract may permit the university to have a great deal of input in daily operations, managerial and advisory issues must be identified and negotiated as part of the original contract.

Costs Differential. Many factors contribute to higher student service costs at metropolitan institutions. First, the cost-of-living index is generally higher in metropolitan areas than in rural areas, so costs of supplies, services, and equipment are higher. Second, the competition for both professional and support staff drives salary levels higher than at institutions in rural communities without larger worker and industrial bases. Third, most metropolitan campuses are younger in age than rural institutions, which results in higher start-up costs for programs and services. As an example of this phenomenon, building residence halls is much more expensive now than a generation ago. Additionally, institutions with a longer history can benefit from a larger and more successful alumni and donor base.

Finally, metropolitan universities find that the cost of providing services is higher than at residential campuses because of higher drop-out and stop-out rates and the lower average credit hour enrollment of metropolitan students. It can cost just as much to provide services (such as advising and counseling) for students taking six or nine hours as it does for students taking fifteen or more hours. Furthermore, services are expended to prepare students for the given semester, and when they drop out additional students have to be recruited to replace those who left. A larger headcount is usually needed at metropolitan universities to generate the same number of credit hours as for traditional students engaged in a steady pattern of full-time enrollment. This has significant implications on the tuition and fee income levels and expenditures for necessary student services.

Accountability. The need to create an accountability system grew more prevalent in higher education in the 1990s. As a result of public criticism given the cost of tuition and public support dollars, institutions have been asked to justify their results. Student affairs units are under closer scrutiny because of a historical dearth of outcomes measurements. Whereas academic units can reflect credit hours, student enrollments, and publications produced by the faculty, student affairs units have no such measurements in terms of the value of each unit. Student affairs units are under increasing pressure to develop outcome measurements, probably in line with the suggestion provided by the Student Learning Imperative of the American College Personnel Association (1994). Assessment tools that indicate the contributions made by student affairs functions to student learning and development assist student affairs divisions in articulating their case for additional resources and institutional power.

Student affairs divisions in metropolitan universities and colleges are also under pressure to provide outcomes measurements given the lower rates of student retention and graduation at these institutions.

Conclusion

Student affairs units at metropolitan campuses share many of the same issues faced by their counterparts at other universities and colleges. Organizational changes, staffing levels, and financial resources are all concerns to student affairs staff. Metropolitan campuses face unique issues involving the pressure to provide services to a diversifying student population while available resources are declining. At the same time, new delivery systems such as off-campus sites and distance learning programs are adding costs to services.

Student affairs divisions in metropolitan universities are, in some ways, better able to meet the challenges facing higher education today. The metropolitan community affords more opportunities to find local consultants, and to interact with elected officials who may provide assistance to the institution. Greater options are available for students, faculty, and staff to perform practical outreach activities as practice that combines academic learning with skill development.

Metropolitan campuses, with their nontraditional student populations, continue to be attractive to students, faculty, and staff. Institutional planning that includes leaders from student affairs can assist in developing appropriate organizational, staffing, and financial plans.

References

American College Personnel Association. *The Student Learning Imperative: Implications for Student Affairs.* Washington, D.C.: American College Personnel Association, 1994.

Brinkman, D. T. (ed.). *Conducting Interinstitutional Comparisons.* New Directions for Institutional Research, no. 53. San Francisco: Jossey-Bass, 1987.

Brinkman, P., and Krakower, J. *Comparative Data for Administrators in Higher Education.* Boulder, Colo.: National Center for Higher Education Management Systems, 1983.

Caruthers, J. K., and Orwig, M. *Budgeting in Higher Education.* (AAHE-ERIC/Higher Education Research Report No.9). Washington, D.C.: American Association of Higher Education, 1981.

Gaither, G., and DeWitt, R. "Making Tough Choices: Retrenchment and Reallocations During Hard Times." *NACUBO Business Officer,* Aug. 1991, pp. 21–24.

Ginsburg, M. H. "An Analysis of Student Affairs Budget Allocation Practices from 1984 to 1988 at Urban Public Research Universities." Unpublished doctoral dissertation, Department of Educational Leadership and Policy Studies, Loyola University of Chicago, 1993.

Lozier, G. G., and Althouse, P. R. "Developing Planning and Budgeting Strategies for Internal Recycling of Funds." *Research in Higher Education,* 1983, *18,* 237–250.

Meisinger, R. J., and Dubeck, L. W. *College and University Budgeting: An Introduction for Faculty and Academic Administrators.* Washington, D.C.: National Association of College and University Business Officers, 1984.

Pembroke, W. J. "Fiscal Constraints on Program Development." In M. J. Barr and L. A. Keating (eds.), *Developing Effective Student Services Programs.* San Francisco: Jossey-Bass, 1985.

Pfeffer, J. *Organizations and Organization Theory.* Marshfield, Mass.: Pitman, 1982.

Schuh, J. H. (ed.). *Financial Management for Student Affairs Administrators.* Alexandria, Va.: American College Personnel Association, 1990.

Vandament, W. E. *Managing Money in Higher Education.* San Francisco: Jossey-Bass, 1989.

Wildavsky, A. B. *The Politics of the Budgetary Process.* (4th ed.). New York: Little, Brown, 1984.

MICHAEL GINSBURG is associate vice-chancellor for student affairs and enrollment management and assistant professor of education at the University of Illinois at Chicago.

*Metropolitan universities pose unique challenges and opportunities
for student affairs professionals. The characteristics of the students
tend to reflect the diversity of the population in the surrounding region.
Building a campus community, getting extremely diverse and busy
students involved in campus life, and effectively responding to student
needs are especially challenging in the urban setting.*

Challenges and Opportunities

*Caryl K. Smith, Virginia D. Gauld, LeVester Tubbs,
with assistance from Richard Correnti*

Student affairs professionals at metropolitan universities have unique challenges and opportunities in contemporary higher education. The composition
of the student body at a metropolitan university tends to reflect the diversity
of the general population of its surrounding region. Certain characteristics are
consistent among the student populations. The student body represents a variety of ethnic and racial groups, includes both residential and commuter students, has a substantial percentage of commuters, and includes a broad range
of age groups. Many students at metropolitan universities take more than four
years to attain a baccalaureate degree and often attend more than one institution in the process. Commonly they are employed, and a steadily increasing
proportion of students attend part-time (Lynton, 1995).

Undergraduate students at a metropolitan university are likely to work at
least part-time while enrolled, to attend school part-time, and to have significant
family responsibilities. The student body also may contain many students who
are the first in their family to attend college and many who have come to the
university with specific career-related goals. It is imperative that student affairs
professionals share information about these students with the faculty and staff,
so that the entire campus community realizes the unique natures of the metropolitan university students.

Emphasizing the benefits of an active campus life for these students is a
significant challenge for the student affairs professionals on metropolitan campuses. Throughout this chapter, examples of successful strategies, programs,
and resources are presented as models for meeting this challenge.

Who Are the Students?

Demographics. The undergraduate profile at a metropolitan university varies widely in age, from the teenage secondary school student earning college credit to people of retirement age following courses they never had a chance to take. The Education Resources Institute (TERI) of the Institute for Higher Education Policy, in the 1996 report *Life After Forty,* states that "students over 40, the fastest growing age cohort in postsecondary education, represent a new set of opportunities and challenges for the nation's system of postsecondary education and training" (p. 9). Most students over forty attend classes on a part-time basis and have difficulty taking advantage of student services designed to assist them; they have better grades than younger students but take longer to complete their studies (Institute for Higher Education Policy, 1996).

Many metropolitan university students live at home with their parents, their spouses, or other relatives and commute to the campus up to five times a week. At the University of Akron, a survey of first-year students revealed that more than one-half (50.9 percent) lived with their parents, a spouse, or a committed partner, while more than one-third (37.2 percent) lived off campus with friend(s) or roommate(s) (University of Akron, 1995b).

Looking at the description of these students, we understand that they prefer to have higher education available to them in the areas where they live. Restrictions on mobility diminish the range of choices for many students. Instead of looking at state, regional, or national options, the marketplace for these students is the immediate metropolitan area in which they reside. Commuter students often drive significant distances to reach campus. The Akron survey (1995b) revealed that 53 percent of the freshmen commuters drove more than ten miles each way and 24.2 percent drove more than twenty-one miles each way.

Many metropolitan universities, when compared with other public institutions of similar size, provide housing for a relatively small proportion of the total student population on campus. Some urban schools are just now beginning to provide on-campus housing, while others are faced with costly renovations of older existing facilities, and some others are expanding the types of housing facilities available to students. The new and renovated facilities tend to be either apartment or suite-style accommodations with fiber-optic and cable installations included.

Minority students represent a significant aspect of life at a metropolitan university. Depending on the location of the institution, the ethnic student population differs in composition and size in relation to the total student body. At Florida International University (FIU), a large public university, the minority student population is more than one-half of the total enrolled students. Half of FIU's student population is Hispanic; three-quarters of these students are Cuban-American. In addition, 15 percent of the student body is African American, and there are almost two thousand international students. FIU seeks to create a comfortable environment for this very diverse student body through support services and programs. However, *The Chronicle of Higher Education* recently reported that the Hispanic students at FIU can no longer qualify for scholarships that the university reserves for minority students. How this matter will be adjudicated by the institution and the courts is yet to be determined.

In the Southwest, a similar situation has occurred as both the student population of the University of New Mexico and the population of the entire state have become "majority-minority." This occurs when a population group recognized as minority numerically becomes the largest group.

Enrollment Patterns. Since 1987, the Public Urban Universities Student Affairs Data Exchange reports (1996) that most metropolitan universities have between 25 and 45 percent of their undergraduate students enrolled part-time. This large part-time population not only impacts the total credit hours produced—usually a major factor in state funding for the public institutions—but it obviously has a direct impact on the graduation rates of these universities. Data indicate that most metropolitan universities do not reach a 40 percent graduation rate until eight or nine years after first enrollment.

The six metropolitan universities in Ohio (University of Akron, University of Cincinnati, Cleveland State University, University of Toledo, Wright State University, and Youngstown State University), all members of the Public Urban Universities, commonly known as the Urban 13+ institutions, reported retention rates generally above the national average for the period from fall 1994 to fall 1995, when compared with other doctoral-degree granting universities with similar levels of admissions selectivity. The Ohio Inter-University Council Student Affairs Committee report (1996) is based on data for all full-time, new first-year students. The six Ohio universities, with the exception of the University of Cincinnati, self-identify their admissions policy as "open." The first-to-second-year institutional retention rates ranged from 62 percent for Cleveland State to 70 percent for the universities of Akron and Toledo. The University of Cincinnati, which defines its admissions policy as ranging from open to highly selective, had a retention rate of 75 percent, which was difficult to compare to the national data (Ohio Inter-University Council Student Affairs Committee, 1996, and American College Testing Program, 1995).

The University of Akron (UA) conducted a survey of students who did not return to school the following semester when they were academically eligible to do so. It revealed that a considerable number of students did not feel that they had "dropped out" but rather reported that they had to stay out to earn more money so that they could return the *next* term. This in-and-out enrollment pattern, based on circumstances of work and one's financial wherewithal, is an important consideration for institutional planners and for those who try to communicate with current and prospective students, both new and returning.

Graduation rates for metropolitan universities often appear low to the casual observer, until the substantial numbers of part-time students are taken into account. The Public Urban Universities Student Affairs Data Exchange reports that there is approximately a 20 percent difference in retention between full-time students and part-time students for each of four years beginning with the 1990 class of first-time freshmen. For example, after one year, the full-time men who entered in fall 1990 were retained at a rate of nearly 70 percent, while the part-time men were retained at nearly 50 percent. Similar findings also were shown for full-time and part-time women. The report also indicates that there does not appear to be a direct relationship between commuting and either retention or graduation rates (Public Urban Universities Student Affairs Data Exchange, 1996).

Most metropolitan universities have a sizable number of course offerings after 4:00 P.M. This is an important option for institutions to consider in planning how to accommodate students who work and attend school, as this type of scheduling appeals to substantial numbers of students. In 1995–96 data, Georgia State University reported that more than eighty-six hundred students attended at 4:00 P.M. or later. Both the University of Akron and Indiana University/Purdue University at Indianapolis reported having more than six thousand attending at that hour or later.

Financial Sources of Funding College. The federal government, through a wide variety of programs, is the largest source of funding available to assist students and their families. Metropolitan university students are no exception. Institutionally provided funding and commercial lenders are other major providers of financial assistance. Over the last twenty years, the balance of the types of student financial aid provided from these sources has reversed. Formerly, most student aid was in the form of grants and scholarships, with less provided by loans. Now, the most common source of aid for students or their parents is in loan monies, with comparatively little coming from grants or scholarships, whatever the sources of the funding.

In a study of how undergraduate students finance their education, conducted by UA in 1995, of those who responded, more 47 percent had taken out loans to help meet their college expenses. A large percentage of these students estimated that the debt accumulated over the course of their college careers would exceed $10,000. It is no wonder that some financial experts refer to this obligation as a type of reverse dowry that these students carry into their after-college lives.

The UA study showed that 75.7 percent of the respondents were working at the time of the survey, and an additional 10.2 percent had worked previously while enrolled. Of those working, a surprising 22.9 percent held two jobs, and 2.6 percent held three or more jobs while attending school. Of the same group, 27.7 percent reported working thirty-six or more hours per week. Among those who worked that many hours, 24 percent were enrolled full-time, taking twelve semester credit hours or more. It was interesting to note that students aged twenty-five or over worked significantly longer hours than those students who were under that age.

It is amazing to imagine how a student works multiple jobs and attends school at the same time. The implications of this survey for campus life are enormous. It is no wonder that student affairs professionals often are frustrated when trying to interest these highly motivated but very busy students in becoming involved in more aspects of campus life.

In what one can assume is a common situation for students at other metropolitan universities, the Akron students in the aforementioned survey reported that few of their college expenses are paid by their family (when compared with similar nationwide data). Many students expressed frustration about parental contributions. The national statistics indicate that 44 percent of college students have all expenses paid by their family, while only 12.4 percent made that claim in the Akron survey. On the other hand, 46.5 percent of the Akron students indicated that they received *no* financial help from the family, while nationally there were 27 percent who received no family support for college (University of Akron, 1995a).

What Is the Campus Diversity Picture at Metropolitan Universities?

Metropolitan universities often have an ethnically diverse student body, since most urban areas in the United States have an ethnically diverse population and metropolitan universities serve these cities. It is important for a metropolitan university to understand the ethnic makeup of its urban area and determine if it is responding to the community's diverse needs. A metropolitan university must use this information in recruitment. Within each ethnic group, what is the high-school graduation rate? How many students are college bound? How many older adults are coming to college? Are birth rates increasing?

The university must also look at its own internal figures. How many students of each ethnic group are currently enrolled? What is their average age? What are their rates of retention and graduation? How many faculty and staff members belong to each ethnic group? Does the percentage of faculty and staff from various ethnic groups reflect the percentage of students in the same groups?

Recruitment and Retention. Once an institution declares its commitment to attracting and retaining a diverse student enrollment, and after it assesses the needs of the student population and evaluates its current performance in addressing those needs, then it can determine if changes are needed. This process was used at the University of Alabama at Birmingham (UAB) several years ago. Under the leadership of a visionary president, UAB declared a commitment to increase the number of African Americans completing Ph.D.s and first professional degrees. Analysis indicated that there was an inadequate pool of African American faculty available throughout the United States. Institutions of higher education were locked in a bidding war with one another to recruit African Americans to their faculty. At UAB, it was determined that a pipeline should be established that would begin with high school students and make financial commitments from high school to the undergraduate, graduate, and faculty levels. The president made a major financial commitment to this effort, using funds from the state appropriation.

The high school program focuses primarily on summer programs for African American students and provides a structured experience in UAB research labs, where the students are mentored by UAB faculty. The program lasts eight weeks and includes college-preparatory seminars that emphasize cognitive and affective learning skills. Participants come from the Birmingham area and are either high school juniors or seniors. Each student receives a stipend and is eligible to compete for undergraduate scholarships at UAB.

The undergraduate program provides scholarship assistance throughout the four years of undergraduate school. For summer study, full tuition, fees, and a stipend are provided for approximately seventy-five students in a research lab with a faculty mentor. Students must participate in a series of seminars sponsored by the Office of Minority Recruitment and Retention and are encouraged to interact with one another as well as to participate in leadership activities on the campus. The retention and graduation rates of these students significantly exceed the overall graduation rate of the general undergraduate population. A significant number of the matriculants have gone on to graduate or professional school programs.

Fellowships and mentoring are the foundations of the graduate student program. Assistance is offered to encourage students to present papers at professional meetings in order to establish themselves in their fields. Mentors meet frequently with these graduate students to assess progress, offer support, and make appropriate referrals for help as needed. Emphasis is on the holistic development of the student.

In order to increase the number of African American faculty at UAB, a financial set-aside was implemented. This gives the deans an incentive to increase the number of African American faculty in their schools. A plan also was developed to assist minority faculty members who were completing their dissertations and to assist young faculty in getting appropriately established and making satisfactory progress toward tenure.

In summary, this is a long-term project which has already impacted positively on the climate of this campus. The percentage of African American faculty at UAB was 2.9 percent at the beginning of the project; it is now 4.1 percent. The percentage of African American students, especially at the undergraduate levels, has continued to increase. In fall 1990, 26 percent of entering students were African American; in fall 1996, the number was 34 percent.

The program has its critics, especially amid growing concern over affirmative action and quotas. However, the commitment of this institution results in providing greater numbers of African American faculty for institutions of higher education. The efforts at UAB communicate a more welcoming climate for the African American community, which constitutes 37 percent of the population of both the state of Alabama and the greater metropolitan area of Birmingham.

A Welcoming Environment. Once the institutional commitment is made to recruit and retain a diverse student population, a plan for comfortable interaction between diverse groups should be developed. One way to create a welcoming environment is to have support services that emphasize the holistic development of all students. These programs may include tutoring, developmental advising, and student organizational support. Some institutions create "home bases" for various groups so that they have a location where they can be together with students of their own ethnic or racial origin. In an institution as diverse as Florida International University, the challenge to create a welcoming, comfortable environment has been significant. FIU has not only focused on support services for currently enrolled students but also emphasized precollege programs. Working in cooperation with the Dade County schools and churches, the university has been awarded Ford Foundation and Upward Bound grants, which allow it to provide services primarily to junior and senior high school students with programs such as "Switch On to Math and Science."

A similar collaborative summer program exists between UAB and Girls, Inc. The "Eureka!" program started as a collaborative effort between Brooklyn College and Girls, Inc., to work with middle school female students. The program was expanded about three years ago, and Girls, Inc., of Birmingham and UAB received funding to establish a similar program. The program primarily identifies African American girls who have demonstrated math, science, and technology aptitude and who also were projected as likely high-school dropouts unless intervention occurred. The curriculum includes exposure to research and computer labs, leadership seminars, and a major emphasis on developing good individual and team sports skills. These students are being tracked as they progress through high school to determine their continuation through higher education and their success in the sciences and technology.

Support services are key both to successful retention of diverse students and to comfortable interaction between ethnic and racial groups. Encouraging groups to celebrate their history throughout the year and inviting members of other racial and ethnic groups to attend these programs helps these groups to value one another. For example, by starting with the celebration of Black History Month and then expanding activities throughout the year, an institution can demonstrate its commitment to black history and to the presence of black leaders on campus as positive role models for all students. Other programs, such as Hispanic heritage and American Heritage festivals, emphasize the university's commitment to traditions and customs of other ethnic groups. Many metropolitan universities, for example, are sponsoring Kwanzaa programs during the winter to celebrate the African American heritage.

The fraternity and sorority systems can contribute to racial fragmentation on campus. Care must be taken to encourage these groups to be inclusive rather than exclusive. For example, if a campus has member organizations of the National Panhellenic Conference, National Pan-Hellenic Council, and National Interfraternity Conference, it is important that an umbrella council with representation from all groups be established and that leadership be offered to encourage interaction. These groups should work together to cohost Order of Omega awards, plan membership recruitment activities, and support those groups that might not have large numbers of participants. Seminars sponsored jointly by this umbrella council can demonstrate campus commitment to collaborative interaction.

International Students. As more international students seek to study at American metropolitan universities, an understanding of the major countries sending their students to the United States is important. An institution must determine if it is going to aggressively recruit international students, on which countries it will focus its efforts, and whether it is able to articulate with international coursework as well as provide support services to facilitate the international students' transition to the campus in the United States. At UAB, where more than one thousand international students representing more than eighty countries are enrolled, the Center for International Programs is the coordinating group for all international students. Information about immigration status is provided by this team of professionals, as is a "safe haven" atmosphere. A thorough orientation program is required of all international students to ensure that policies and procedures are communicated. In addition, currently enrolled international students provide a more personal orientation for new international students to help them with pragmatic concerns such as where to shop, how to establish a bank account, and where to go for entertainment.

The UAB's Smolian House is an example of how, through the commitment of a generous family who were focused on the importance of embracing internationalism, an urban university could construct a facility to bring domestic and international students together. This facility is not just a home away from home for the international students and their families. It also serves as a place where domestic students can meet with students from many cultures and share their cultures, while addressing their differences. Formal and informal activities take place to encourage international students not to isolate from domestic students. This facility also offers classes such as English as a second language to international students and family members who wish to participate. A short-term residency floor allows international students to live there briefly if they are locating permanent housing or do not need long-term housing. A graduate assistant oversees this facility along with a full-time professional staff member who develops support services for international students as well as programs to encourage interaction between domestic and international students. The facility has also been significantly supported by the Rotary Club of Birmingham and has provided a way for this urban university to interact with these community leaders through mutual international interests.

The UAB's successful Interculture program, which is led by a student committee, focuses on building partnerships between international and domestic students. The Smolian House sponsors monthly programs to highlight traditions and holidays of different ethnic groups. It also sponsors a fall barbecue for international students and their families to welcome them to the campus.

Students with Disabilities. Following passage of the Americans with Disabilities Act, many metropolitan universities are experiencing an increase in the enrollment of students who are physically or mentally challenged. A clear understanding of the requirements for compliance with the Act is imperative, since the support services provided for these students are frequently housed within student affairs operations. Care must be taken that this unit not become the only office understanding the needs and expectations of students with disabilities. A coordinating committee comprising representatives of the legal office, architectural and engineering design services, and faculty should work with the disabilities support service office to advise the institution of any problems existing on the campus. This group might develop a seminar for faculty and staff about the Americans with Disabilities Act and institutional policies and procedures for providing reasonable accommodations to students. The entire institution must understand the obligation to accommodate qualified students with disabilities, and understand that these accommodations are individually arranged and can be expensive.

The problems that occur are frequently related to nonphysical, less apparent psychological or learning disabilities. A system should be developed for alerting faculty about students who are entitled to reasonable accommodations. The disabilities support service office should provide a method for answering questions from faculty about accommodation. The legal office of the university can serve as a mediating resource to help resolve any questions that arise regarding reasonable accommodations.

In order to establish a positive climate on campus for students with disabilities, programs should be offered to help faculty, staff, and students appreciate these students. For example, universities could celebrate the week set aside for disabilities awareness. Featuring success stories of physically challenged students in campus publications can be a powerful tool as well.

Age Diversity. Another challenging diversity issue on the metropolitan campus is the age diversity of undergraduate students. It is not unusual to have a class with many students above age twenty-two, and even a significant number over fifty. A common factor among all the older students is likely to be that the majority of them work while going to school. This raises several issues. Adult students have multiple demands on their time, energy, and thought. As a consequence, adult students need and expect courses to be offered in formats and at times that respond to their needs. They differ from full-time, traditional-age students who are focused on their college experience and, as young adults, are more often willing to be directed by adult faculty and administrators. The adult student, on the other hand, frequently wants to be on a more equal playing field with administrators and faculty. A key question often raised by adult students is whether they are truly welcomed on the campus or just tolerated.

Metropolitan universities understand the importance of providing services to students from many age groups. Classes offered in extended weekend, evening, or early morning formats are numerous. Special orientation sessions for adult students can focus on the unique needs of this segment of the student population. Support groups and organizations, such as women's centers or adult student organizations, can help identify the unique needs of adults and help the institution be responsive. Career centers frequently offer assessment and advising for adults who are changing careers or seeking upward mobility.

At some metropolitan universities, there are offices specifically established to facilitate services for adult students. Many of these offices were developed based on the definitive work done by Patricia Cross (1979) and Arthur Chickering (Chickering and Associates, 1989). Having the capability to assess work accomplishments and help adults identify what they can apply from their work experience to the curriculum can save valuable time and money for many adult students. These offices can also represent the needs of adult students to faculty and provide support services through extended hours and formats appropriate for adults. Out-of-class learning opportunities planned for adult students with children can demonstrate the institution's commitment to provide services to students from older age groups.

The overarching question that must be answered by the metropolitan university is this: Does the institution truly welcome diversity? Once the question is answered affirmatively, the institution must clearly articulate this commitment. What does each unit of the institution do each year to celebrate diversity? Is care taken to ensure a diverse workforce at all levels of the institution? When committees are formed for planning and decision making, is there a focus on being sure that a diverse group is chosen? If the institution declares its mission to proactively recruit and retain a diverse student body, then diverse faculty and staff should develop a plan for how this mission is to be accomplished and an assessment method to evaluate and celebrate its success.

What Is Campus Student Life at Metropolitan Universities?

Student populations often appear to be less involved at metropolitan universities than at other institutions. Several factors might explain this phenomenon. Especially for commuters, being a student is only one of many demanding roles and responsibilities in their lives. As mentioned earlier, commuters work full-time or part-time. Many also have responsibilities for managing households and caring for children, siblings, or other relatives. With their limited time, commuter students often have to select their campus involvement carefully. The relative value of an activity is usually a major factor in their involvement. Obviously, these students usually require complete and timely information about campus opportunities (Jacoby, 1995). If a school has a higher number of commuters than residential students, there will probably be less campus involvement. This can lead to the appearance that the students are apathetic.

Apparent apathy also could be due to the many social, cultural, and intellectual opportunities existing in a metropolitan environment. With this variety of activities, students easily become much more involved in off-campus events and culture. Even though metropolitan universities can and do have large student populations, the number is relatively small compared with the total number of people in an urban environment. This leads to another problem these institutions must face: there are usually other higher education institutions within the metropolitan area. For example, in Denver's metro area there are twenty-two institutions of higher education. The college or university with the most popular activities, creative personnel, and quality facilities often attracts students from other schools to their programs.

Building a Sense of Campus Community. The characteristics of the students and the complex urban environment provide a context of diversity and change that challenges metropolitan universities. Social change, demographic shifts in population, and an ever-evolving economic environment all contribute to the setting in which these universities function (Barnett and Phares, 1995). Metropolitan universities seem to be more open-minded than nonurban universities thanks to the great variety of people, culture, places, and activities that surround it. Higher education institutions need to capitalize on what occurs culturally in the community as well as at other universities in the metropolitan area to create cooperative programs.

A sense of community develops on campus whether planned or not. It may be experienced by campus citizens, both staff and students, as positive or negative. Obviously, the goal is to create the most positive experience possible. Fostering a sense of belonging is an important element in developing a campus community. Numerous activities can contribute to this sense of belonging: athletics, social activities, clubs and organizations, campus entertainment, topical seminars and speakers, active student governing boards, and student honoraries and honor societies.

Florida International University has thirty honor societies, mostly through their academic programs, that assist in getting students involved in academic interest areas. At the University of Central Florida (UCF), the student affairs administration deliberately places emphasis on Greek organizations as a way of creating a sense of community. With a small residential population, developing a Greek system fosters the development of a *collegiate environment,* as well as a sense of community for a predominantly commuter campus. The Greek system has provided a majority of student leadership and has been instrumental in student government, the campus activities board, the orientation program, and countless other student organizations. Although student involvement in Greek organizations has declined nationally, at UCF it has seen steady growth. Much of this can be attributed to administrative support. At UCF, Greek Affairs operates out of the dean of students' office rather than the student activities office as is typical of most schools. This organizational structure has led to the largest modern Greek housing development in the country. Another example of efforts to increase or develop a sense of community at UCF was a mock presidential debate recently sponsored by Pi Sigma Alpha, a political science honor society.

An office of student activities can provide worthwhile activities to build a sense of campus community by bridging differences, building partnerships, increasing tolerance, and enhancing global perspectives. At UCF, the Campus Activities Board is responsible for providing entertainment that suits the needs of the entire student population. For example, the board provided speakers for special events such as sexual awareness week, showed movies for students and their friends or family, and coordinated programs by Consultants for Effective Leadership. This last is a group of trained student leaders who help student organizations improve their organizational skills and operations.

Universities can increase the sense of campus community in a variety of ways. Building partnerships with the surrounding community is important. Career resource centers, for example, provide an excellent opportunity for community partnerships. Career centers allow employers to recruit candidates for jobs directly from campus, for both part-time and full-time jobs. UCF has developed a unique partnership with Lockheed Martin that employs 160–200 students. In 1995, the total contract was $1.7 million, with $1.4 million going to students as salaries and approximately $300,000 to the university for administrative fees.

Residential and Commuter Students. Commuter students make up more than 80 percent of today's students in American colleges and universities. About 54 percent of these live off campus but not with parents, while 27 percent live with one or both parents. No matter what their educational goals are, where they live, or what type of institution they attend, the fact that they commute has a profound influence on their collegiate experience. Major studies have shown that these students are at greater risk of attrition and have less overall satisfaction with whatever college they attend (Jacoby, 1995).

Residence halls have been an important part of American higher education since its beginnings. Even at predominantly commuter schools, the tradition of residential life has been responsible for developing attitudes, policies, and practices. Because of the convenience of living on campus and the staff support available, residential students often have an advantage over commuter students in terms of opportunities for personal growth and development, better grades and graduation rates, and a more satisfying experience with the institution. Resident students often have more opportunities to attend activities; have more access to facilities, resources, and faculty; tend to become more involved; and gain more leadership skills through this involvement. Since commuter students divide their time between classes, commuting, work, and family obligations, they may not be able to experience the same opportunities as resident students.

Developing commuters' sense of belonging is an important function of colleges and universities. This can be achieved by providing some basic facilities such as lockers and lounge areas in several campus locations, which enables students to develop relationships with fellow students, faculty, and staff. Some suitable areas for this environment are libraries, student unions and centers, and athletic or exercise facilities. Developing significant relationships enhances the likelihood that commuter students can develop a feeling of being connected to the institution (Jacoby, 1995).

Student Union or Student Center. Student unions can provide excellent facilities where all students have socialization opportunities and can gain a feeling of connection to the institution. When developing a model for a student union, administrators should address such needs as reading and study rooms, computer rooms, food courts with a variety of foods, extended hours, and security officers. A variety of programming opportunities on timely topics should be consistently implemented, with awareness of all the activities available in the immediate metropolitan environment.

Metropolitan universities face unique challenges regarding the services offered in their student unions. Even though all students usually pay a student activities fee, it is the resident student who usually uses student unions and is more likely to participate in student activities (Coles, 1995). Richard Correnti, vice president for student affairs at Florida International University, says "the student union/center is a big part of campus community building, and needs a major commitment to keep it up and running well" (personal communication, Nov. 2, 1996). FIU has spent $21 million in expanding the main campus student center over the past eight years, in addition to $5.5 million to develop a student center at a branch campus.

Traditionally, many of the features of a student union are directed toward the residential student population. To better accommodate commuter students, these unions should offer options and services to meet their needs, such as lockers and lounge spaces that can provide a base of operations when they are between classes. These buildings should be equipped to handle heavier traffic during the day but also provide the necessary services to evening and weekend students that enable them to feel part of the campus community. Student unions should offer spaces for meetings and other campus and public functions. These facilities should be competitive in design and price with similar facilities within the metropolitan area.

Building Relationships. Pascarella and Terenzini (1991) concluded that the environmental and contextual conditions of a college were as important to student involvement in learning activities as were programmatic variables. The two most important factors with student learning are, first, the frequency and quality of students' relationships with institutional agents and peers, and second the time and effort students devote to various activities such as studying and interacting with faculty and peers about academic matters, including the degree that students take.

Studies reveal that peer relations are as important to student learning as are relationships with faculty. Encouraging this peer interaction is difficult at a metropolitan university because commuter students tend to be so busy. A metropolitan university may want to take steps to encourage informal interaction between students. Some steps include scheduling guest lectures over the noon hour or requiring attendance for certain speakers or events as part of a course grade. Additionally, using small groups for discussion both during class time and out-of-class is a way to encourage peer interaction (Arnold, Kuh, Vesper, and Schuh, 1993).

Other ways a metropolitan university can promote environmental interaction among students, faculty, and staff include developing a faculty and staff programming directory for students' use; offering social hours with students in the halls and unions; meeting with department heads and deans regarding development of connections between faculty and the department of student affairs; involving students and faculty as team members on committees and volunteer projects; asking faculty to facilitate study groups and leadership training days; and inviting faculty to speak with students about their hobbies, studies abroad, or political concerns.

Safety and Security. The federal Student Right-to-Know and Campus Security Act of 1990 has caused universities to report to the campus community and other interested parties on crimes occurring on campus. This has brought about an increase in concern for the precautions and security measures taken on campuses across the United States.

Since metropolitan universities are located in suburban and urban environments, it follows that much of what occurs in that environment is paralleled on campus. Crime on campus can be a reflection of its surrounding area. Security is a particular concern for students at a metropolitan university. It is the responsibility of the university to provide a campus that is as safe and secure as possible and that is conducive to a learning environment. Restricted access areas, electronic surveillance, pedestrian escort services, and increased staffing levels for campus patrols are just a few examples of the actions campuses have taken to provide as much security as possible.

Berthiaume (1994) recommends several campus safety enhancement strategies:

- Establish a campus safety and security task force comprising faculty, staff, students, and campus police administrators to monitor and find ways to enhance campus safety.
- Ensure that the campus maintains compliance with both the 1990 Student Right-to-Know and Campus Security Act and recent legislative action.
- Require annual safety- and security-related in-service training for all institutional employees, regardless of rank or tenure.
- Survey students, faculty, staff, and visitors regarding their assessment of campus safety.
- Hire an outside consultant to review the strengths and weaknesses of campus safety procedures, and attitudes in this regard.
- Provide support and direction for the development of five-year and ten-year action plans pertaining to campus safety and security issues.
- Ensure that the campus has open lines of communication and good working relationships with the local and state police departments.
- Inspect campus facilities and grounds to identify high-risk areas. Shrubbery should be trimmed to appropriate heights, ground floor windows and doors should be secured, and electronic access systems should be installed where appropriate.

Increasing Student Retention. Evening and weekend programs appear to be of major interest to students in the urban university. Considering the characteristics of many nontraditional students, this is not surprising. The decline in enrollment of the traditional college age population has caused many colleges and universities to evaluate their course offerings carefully in order to attract a larger number of adults and nontraditional students. Even though enrollment of these students has increased, many academic and student service programs have not been adjusted to meet those students' needs and to help them succeed in meeting their academic goals.

Most universities provide extended office hours to accommodate nontraditional students. Essential student service offices, such as admissions, records and registration, financial aid, counseling and testing, and others, that provide basic information are often open later than 5:00 P.M. at least part of each week. Many universities now register and enroll students by telephone and permit payment of fees by credit card in order to provide student-friendly service.

Studies conducted at schools such as the University of Central Florida demonstrate students' desire that more services be provided in a time frame that is useful for them. In one survey (Lawson and Shields, 1996), some students recommended extending professors' office hours, as well as providing greater access to student financial aid, academic advising, registration, on-campus evening child care, public transportation, athletic services, recreation and intramural programs, and access to minority affairs. Issues and concerns of students at this university are consistent with those of students at most metropolitan universities.

Challenges

Many of the challenges for student affairs professionals at metropolitan universities are primarily student-driven. As we have seen, the composition of the student body is diverse. The students, their academic goals, their personal circumstances, and their needs and interests are all factors resulting in challenges for the campus. The challenges and the opportunities that they provide for the staff at metropolitan universities determine the strategic planning efforts, daily experiences, and campus climate of these higher education institutions. Challenges include:

- Delivering student services and programs by methods and at times that appeal to widely divergent student schedules.
- Developing effective means to communicate with commuter students and assist them with the information they need to make the institution function for them.
- Providing financial assistance for students who might not qualify for traditional types of aid, such as developing student emergency loan funds when none currently exist or establishing scholarships specifically for part-time undergraduate students.
- Encouraging student organizations to adapt their programs to accommodate students who are not "traditional" in demographic terms.

- Establishing a variety of campus safety nets, or early warning systems, to facilitate timely and academically appropriate intervention for students who do not show signs of succeeding as they begin their academic programs. This initial failure to thrive academically in the campus environment can be especially devastating to a student who is enrolled only part-time.
- Providing opportunities for all students to experience campus life through campus facilities available for study, computer use, informal time with others, and recreation. Such facilities should be conveniently located throughout the campus and well maintained.
- Providing career exploration programs and placement services to assist students in effectively participating in a rapidly changing work world and a job search process that demands individual diligence, creativity, and flexibility.
- Conducting research on students, their needs, their retention and graduation rates, the effectiveness of student services and programs, and the costs of doing our work, and comparing this data, when possible, with peer institutions. These efforts are of invaluable assistance in the continual planning and assessment modes prevalent across higher education today.

Conclusion

Much of what determines the success of students—whether they remain enrolled or not, whether they make satisfactory academic progress and complete degrees—is influenced by personnel, programs, and services in student affairs. Student affairs must help the entire campus understand that retention efforts can only succeed when viewed as a universitywide responsibility. In our review of examples of creative and innovative efforts to increase student satisfaction and retention, it is obvious that many metropolitan universities are meeting the needs of their students well; but challenges and opportunities remain for most institutions.

Given the nature of our students and the mission and history of our metropolitan institutions, we student affairs professionals need to be especially innovative in planning and implementing the programs, services, and resources for students. Our universities must compensate, in general, for having fewer alumni in the state legislature, for being less understood by the publics outside of the immediate institutional service area, and for having only recently developed fundraising efforts to supplement state and federal income. It is important that student affairs professionals continue to develop ways to measure what is done; how well it is done; what campus environmental factors impact students at metropolitan universities; what the student issues are; and how well the student affairs programs, services, and resources serve the campus and the students. Assessment and research efforts must be implemented and strengthened. In times when public higher education is increasingly scrutinized by many external resources, it behooves student affairs professionals to carry on and extend research efforts to guide continuing programs, strategic planning, and future operations.

References

American College Testing Program. *ACT Institutional Data File.* Iowa City, Iowa: American College Testing Program, 1995.

Adamany, D. "The University as Urban Citizen." *Educational Record,* 1992, 73 (2), 6–9.

Arnold, J., Kuh, G., Vesper, N., and Schuh, J. "Student Age and Enrollment Status as Determinants of Learning and Personal Development at Metropolitan Universities." *Journal of College Student Development,* 1993, 34, 11–16.

Astin, A. W. *What Matters in College? Four Critical Years Revisited.* San Francisco: Jossey-Bass, 1993.

Banta, L., and Black, O. *Assessment in Practice: Putting Principles to Work on the College Campus.* San Francisco: Jossey-Bass, 1996.

Barnett, M., and Phares, D. "The Metropolitan Students." In D. Johnson and D. Bell (eds.), *Metropolitan Universities: An Emerging Model in American Higher Education.* Denton: University of North Texas Press, 1995.

Berthiaume, J. "Campus Crime: Is Your Campus Prepared to Meet the Challenge?" *Southern Association for College Student Affairs Newsletter,* 1994, 45, pp. 3, 6.

Chickering, A. W., and Associates. *The Modern American College.* San Francisco: Jossey-Bass, 1989.

Coles, A. "Student Services at Metropolitan Universities." In D. Johnson and D. Bell (eds.), *Metropolitan Universities: An Emerging Model in American Higher Education.* Denton: University of North Texas Press, 1995.

Cross, K. P. "Adult Learners: Characteristics, Needs, and Interests." In R. E. Peterson and Associates, *Lifelong Learning in America: An Overview of Current Practices, Available Resources, and Future Prospects.* San Francisco: Jossey-Bass, 1979.

Curry, C. W. "Student Headcount Data." Assorted, unpublished, separate items. Miami: Division of Student Affairs, Florida International University, 1996.

Donhardt, G. "How Far Will Commuters Travel?" *Planning for Higher Education,* 1996, 25, 34–37.

Elliott, P. G. *The Urban Campus.* Phoenix: Oryx Press, 1994.

The Education Resources Institute. *Life After Forty: A New Portrait of Today's—and Tomorrow's—Postsecondary Students.* Washington, D.C.: Institute for Higher Education Policy, 1996.

Jacoby, B. "Adapting the Institution to Meet the Needs of Commuter Students." In D. Johnson and D. Bell (eds.), *Metropolitan Universities: An Emerging Model in American Higher Education.* Denton: University of North Texas Press, 1995.

Jones, J. D., and Damron, J. *Student Affairs Programs at Universities in Urban Settings.* Washington, D.C.: National Association of State Universities and Land-Grant Colleges, 1987.

Komives, S. R., Woodard, D. B., and Associates. *Student Services: A Handbook for the Profession.* (3rd ed.). San Francisco: Jossey-Bass, 1996.

Lawson, K., and Shields, T. *10 Year Summary Report: The Cycles Survey—a Report on Student Views of Their Lives at the University.* Orlando: Division of Student Affairs, University of Central Florida, 1996.

Lynton, E. "Knowledge and Scholarship." In D. Johnson and D. Bell (eds.), *Metropolitan Universities: An Emerging Model in American Higher Education.* Denton: University of North Texas Press, 1995, p. 87–98.

Migden, J., and Research Committee. *The University of Akron Student Profile 1995–96.* Akron, Ohio: Division of Student Affairs, University of Akron, 1996.

National Association of State Universities and Land-Grant Colleges. *In Brief: 1996 Facts About Public Universities.* Washington, D.C.: National Association of State Universities and Land-Grant Colleges, 1996.

Ohio Inter-University Council Student Affairs Committee. *Retention Issues and Initiatives in Ohio Public Universities.* Columbus: Ohio Inter-University Council, 1996.

Pascarella, E. T., and Terenzini, P. *How College Affects Students: Findings and Insights from Twenty Years of Research.* San Francisco: Jossey-Bass, 1991.

Public Urban Universities Student Affairs Data Exchange. *1995–1996 Reports.* Confidential report. Boulder, Colo.: John Minter Associates, 1996.

University of Akron, Division of Student Affairs Research Committee. "Financing an Undergraduate Education at the University of Akron." Unpublished results of 1995 survey. Akron: Division of Student Affairs Research Committee, University of Akron, 1995a.

University of Akron. *1995 First Year Student Survey: Institutional Question Responses.* Los Angeles: Cooperative Institutional Research Program, University of California at Los Angeles, 1995b.

CARYL K. SMITH, *associate vice president for student affairs (senior student affairs officer) at the University of Akron, is currently serving as the chairperson of the Public Urban Universities Student Affairs Data Exchange.*

VIRGINIA D. GAULD *is vice president for student affairs at the University of Alabama-Birmingham and an associate professor in the Department of Educational Leadership.*

LEVESTER TUBBS *is vice president for student affairs at the University of Central Florida and an associate professor in the College of Education.*

Relationships between university and community occur at several sites, particularly at elementary and secondary schools, nonprofit organizations, government, businesses and corporations, and other colleges and universities. What each has in common is the benefit that accrues for students and communities alike.

Community Relationships and Partnerships

Richard L. Palm, J. Douglas Toma

Location affords the metropolitan university a variety of opportunities to build relationships and partnerships with many organizations and institutions in the surrounding community (Lynton, 1995). Students reap advantages from these opportunities when attending metropolitan universities. They live and work in a socially and culturally diverse setting and enjoy the cultural life and entertainment options of an urban area. Perhaps the greatest asset available, however, is the access metropolitan university students have to opportunities to work and learn at elementary and secondary schools, nonprofit organizations, businesses and corporations, government, and other colleges and universities. This chapter explores these relationships and partnerships between students at the metropolitan universities and urban communities.

Student-community relationships and partnerships on college campuses are growing. Metropolitan universities have long used academic resources, namely faculty and staff, to address problems in the cities (Harkavy and Wiewel, 1995). Increased involvement by students in the community has followed, particularly recently. Astin (1993) has urged universities to develop ways to involve students more in their own learning. Relationships and partnerships between the university and community do just that. In other words, the more students are involved, the better their collegiate experience becomes. Student learning and personal development is greatly enhanced when there are links between classroom activities and out-of-class experiences (Kuh, Schuh, Whitt, and Associates, 1991). Interaction with the community provides students with a bridge between theoretical work in the classroom and the practical issues that organizations—whether businesses, government, or education—address each day. These off-campus experiences not only enhance the professional development of students (Bok, 1982) but encourage student learning. The often difficult task of retention is also served, as involvement in out-of-classroom programs and activities fosters the development that keeps students in school through completion of their degrees (Astin, 1993).

We expect colleges and universities—metropolitan institutions even more so—to contribute their collective expertise to solving societal problems. Effective problem solving, however, comes only in cooperation with communities (Hathaway, Mulhollan, and White, 1995). Student involvement here is essential. Linking students, with their newly attained knowledge and skills, to various needs within the cities is a win-win proposition. Students invest their time and skills in nearby communities and gain valuable insight and experience. Communities accrue eager and able contributors in addressing pressing issues and solving persistent problems. These links also tie into the service activities and community-focused research of metropolitan university faculty and staff (Ramaley, 1995). In effect, these relationships expand the definition of the metropolitan campus to include the surrounding community, while concurrently enhancing available resources for student learning (Coles, 1995).

These partnerships do not necessarily happen on their own. Metropolitan universities must be diligent in seeking varied avenues for student participation in the community, recognizing the learning opportunities connected with each experience (Barnett and Phares, 1995). These universities already offer students the cultural and lifestyle advantages of surrounding cities. In addition, students relate to communities through institutions that enhance their education: churches, theaters, galleries, and clubs. Some students take participation to the level of performing with choirs or theater groups, or serving in internships with performing organizations. They may also take advantage of seasonal activities such as festivals, or annual activities such as trade shows or conventions, that provide forums for student development outside the traditional intellectual and vocational realms. Students develop in countless ways as they progress through the collegiate experience, and these forums assist in educating the whole student.

This chapter focuses on more formal arrangements between the university and other members of the metropolitan community: internships, part-time employment, volunteer programs, service learning, cocurricular activities, and leadership training. Relationships between university and community occur at several sites, particularly at elementary and secondary schools, nonprofit organizations, government, businesses and corporations, and other colleges and universities. What each has in common is the benefit that accrues for students and communities alike.

Nonprofit Organizations

The metropolitan community typically includes many nonprofit institutions and organizations. They range from soup kitchens to symphony orchestras. Usually, a long list of agencies and organizations designed to serve the diverse population of an urban community is easy to identify. By design or necessity, these programs often keep their paid human resources to a minimum. They rely on volunteers to carry out many of their operations and functions, creating a natural opening that metropolitan university students fill in a variety of ways. Students can shape their volunteer activities to gain experience in an area of future vocational interest. They also focus on the social awareness and moral development that comes with involvement in community-based humanitarian projects (Zlotkowski, 1996). Either way, arrangements benefit both agencies and students.

These links between university and community are included under the general heading of service learning. Service learning is based on a deliberate connection between academic coursework and service projects, applying classroom theory to hands-on problems (Lankard, 1995). It occurs in several venues, with the nonprofit sector prevalent. Metropolitan university students enjoy a great advantage over students at schools located elsewhere because of the variety of nonprofit organizations and institutions present in metropolitan areas. Service learning programs are increasingly popular among students (Cooper, 1993) and have the potential to reverse a trend among young adults toward declining inclination to participate in community life (Garman, 1995). These community service projects offer important alternatives to traditional on-campus student activities, injecting seriousness of purpose and meaningfulness into student life. Students learn and grow, and the community's needs are met, as university and community engage in a commitment to a long-term partnership of service learning (Jacoby and Associates, 1996).

Indiana University-Purdue University at Indianapolis (IUPUI) has incorporated service learning into the academic program, forging direct links between classroom and community. Several academic departments—including biology, education, English, psychology, and sociology—encourage students to participate in community projects, which then count toward their program requirements. Psychology 101 students, for example, assist with program activities at an area hospital. In English 450, students write grant proposals and instructional booklets for community agencies.

Many metropolitan universities include professional schools, among them medical schools, engineering colleges, and theological seminaries. Partnerships between institutions and nonprofits offer preprofessional students essential opportunities to examine their assumptions and hone their skills. Like many other arrangements involving the community and university, these mutually beneficial services are commonly formalized and most often endure beyond students' current participation. The services involved in these types of partnerships often draw positive attention within a community because they provide invaluable services for those who may not have the means to secure the same services elsewhere. Associations with nonprofit agencies benefit both students and clients, and they enhance the public image of metropolitan universities.

At the University of Missouri-Kansas City (UMKC), professional schools involve themselves with programs and activities in the greater Kansas City area, integrating students' academic experience with community needs. Professional schools, particularly in the health sciences, traditionally have had extensive community interactions through internships and residencies in university clinics and hospitals. Other student-focused programs, however, expand these interactions between university and community. For example, UMKC business students work in volunteer income tax assistance. In addition, students in several health-related professional fields—dentistry, medicine, nursing, and pharmacy—serve both the urban and suburban communities through free clinics, health fairs, and screenings in elementary and secondary schools, as well as in their clinical internships and residencies.

The richness of the arts in the metropolitan community provides settings for student involvement in music, theater, art, and other creative endeavors. From learning opportunities through performance to administrative responsibilities, metropolitan university students can be involved in a wide spectrum of the arts. Joint relationships of classroom experiences and active participation in internships with orchestras, dance troupes, summer theater, or museums can be valuable components of the college education. Involvement in the creative arts gives students the opportunity to apply their knowledge, skills, and practice in the actual performance arena.

The University of North Carolina-Charlotte and the greater Charlotte community have developed partnerships for the arts. The Mint Museum of Art, the Charlotte Repertory Orchestra, the North Carolina Blumenthal Performing Arts Center, and Paramount Parks are associations between the university and community offering positions in performance and administration in dance, theater, communication, film, music, and art. Some are paid and some are for academic credit, but all contribute to student learning and provide talent and assistance to the arts.

Elementary and Secondary Schools

Metropolitan universities can provide myriad resources for elementary and secondary schools in their community. Urban schools frequently must address a number of difficult issues: violence, desegregation, retrenchment, school and program closure, truancy and dropout, and inclusion and diversity. The metropolitan university, and particularly its students, can provide needed expertise and experience for urban school systems. University students can work with faculty mentors in helping K–12 school teachers and administrators respond to critical concerns. In exchange, these relationships give students hands-on experience while building their individual academic portfolios.

Long-standing student teaching arrangements offer metropolitan universities a foundation from which to build their relationships with the community through involvement in the schools. Although it is principally education majors who are involved in student teaching, opportunities are available for other students to be mentors in school systems. Both opportunities provide support for programs in the schools and build on the skills of the university students. Expansion beyond traditional programs in both urban and suburban schools into magnet schools or charter schools, for instance, provides unique settings for training. Supporting these new models of K–12 education should also serve evolving urban populations more directly and effectively. Having such a number of options available within a large and diverse community provides metropolitan students with an advantage over their counterparts at other schools. They can develop and test their interests and skills in varied settings. Consequently, students gain experiences that stretch their worldview, while allowing them to make more informed career decisions. Finally, these collaborations among metropolitan universities and area school systems are consistent with movements in several areas toward providing students with a "seamless" educational experience, beginning in kindergarten and ending with a college degree (Smith, 1994; McWilliams and Lewis, 1994).

The University of Nebraska at Omaha (UNO) has formed several alliances with Omaha area school districts, enhancing the quality of K–12 education in the metropolitan area while providing UNO students with invaluable experiences. Through the Metropolitan Omaha Educational Consortium, UNO faculty, staff, and students work with area school districts on common high-priority issues. In addition, student teachers from the university are placed in the seven school districts that make up the consortium. A related effort, the CADRE Project, assists newly certified teachers in their professional adjustment.

Government

Urban centers include federal, state, and local government agencies of all types. Students interested in careers in politics or public policy can find a wide range of opportunities to test their ideas and skills. Like work with nonprofit agencies, work with government agencies offers another outlet for service learning. What remains important is that classroom discussion gives way to actual experience drawn from structured activity. Students clerk in courtrooms, serve on election campaigns, conduct citizen surveys, prepare bond proposals, apprentice in public safety departments, and report on policy work at various levels of local, state, regional, and federal agencies. Their involvement provides actual experiences to support classroom programs and continues the traditional responsibility of the university to prepare people to provide civic leadership. The proximity of the agencies and the university also means students can observe government in action and become more informed and active citizens.

Businesses and Corporations

Private enterprises, ranging from small businesses to large corporations, offer seemingly endless opportunities for metropolitan university students to engage in work that tests classroom teaching and their professional portfolios. These relationships take on a variety of forms: paid or unpaid internships, credit or noncredit courses, and part-time or full-time work. They also serve students having a variety of interests and businesses having diverse needs. Students can choose to work in small stores and offices, local or regional companies, or international corporate headquarters. Paid internships also offer the advantage of helping students meet the expenses of their education.

The points of contact for students with the business community are almost unlimited, as exemplified in the programs of the Center for Entrepreneurship at Wichita State University (WSU). On-the-job training is part of all the center's programs. WSU students, particularly those with an interest in starting a business, have many opportunities to connect with business leaders in the Wichita area. These connections take several forms—interviews, case studies, consulting, work experiences, and internships—some of which are for academic credit and some of which are not.

Students at California State University, Fresno have opportunities for academically related, paid work experiences through a cooperative education program. These students have the opportunity to divide their days between classes and full-time or part-time work. The work assignments provide students with a means to fund their education, while serving to validate career choices and enhance postgraduate job opportunities.

Alumni and Alumnae

There usually are a significant number of metropolitan university alumni and alumnae in the surrounding urban area who can be instrumental in arranging for internships and practica for current students. Alumni and alumnae also serve as informal advisors or mentors to students, making students aware of possibilities either in their business or elsewhere in the community. Alumni and alumnae support of "their" university can be a key to creating off-campus opportunities for students. In addition, community members in business, as well as nonprofits, may become even more actively involved with the university through student-focused partnerships. Such involvement might take the form of service on advisory boards or membership in booster groups. They may also become potential donors to the institution. Finally, these associations encourage community members to participate in the intellectual life of the university as guest lecturers and adjunct faculty, with their expertise adding a significant dimension to the classroom experience.

Cleveland State University has more than four hundred alumni available to students in a program called Career Conversations. Students meet with alumni and gain valuable perspectives on preparing for specific careers. The program is an early intervention that assists students to do career planning throughout their college experiences.

Other Colleges and Universities

The population density in metropolitan areas commonly supports a diverse set of postsecondary institutions. Each joins the metropolitan university in serving community needs. There are other four-year institutions, including public and private colleges and universities, with certain schools offering graduate and professional degrees in addition to undergraduate programs. There are both publicly supported and proprietary two-year institutions and technical training institutes. Agreements among these postsecondary institutions, including the metropolitan university, expand the offerings at any one school and enhance the breadth and depth of the programs of study that individual students construct. Expanded curricular opportunities provide schools located in metropolitan areas with a valuable recruiting tool. These arrangements can also increase efficiency, offering individual institutions an opportunity to cut costs.

In St. Louis, a private institution, Washington University, and a public university with an urban mission, University of Missouri-St. Louis, have developed a joint engineering program. The two universities also have cross-course arrangements with several other colleges and universities, both public and private, in the St. Louis area. Similarly, in the Washington, D.C., metropolitan area, twelve colleges and universities join in the Consortium of Universities. The activities of the consortium include cross-registration among its members. These institutions combine their individual strengths to offer broad coursework and experience to students.

In addition, students from both undergraduate and graduate programs at metropolitan universities can arrange practica and internships at neighboring colleges and universities. For instance, graduate students in higher education administration, student affairs, and counseling psychology find these opportunities particularly useful in gaining the knowledge base and practical experience necessary for both entry to their chosen field and advancement within. Interinstitutional arrangements also expose metropolitan university students to different types of institutions. Institutions in turn benefit greatly from having access to these students, who typically bring great energy to their assignments.

Students in the college student personnel services graduate program at the University of Louisville have opportunities to do internships at the seven colleges and universities of the Metroversity Consortium. Training in the urban experience comes through the multiplicity of universities, private colleges, community colleges, and seminaries making up the consortium. Experience within these settings—ranging from the University of Louisville to Bellarmine College, Jefferson Community College, and Louisville Presbyterian Theological Seminary—prepares students for a variety of careers in higher education. Gaining perspectives with hands-on projects in these different settings broadens students' education and enhances their professional portfolios.

The university can enter into partnerships with businesses that conduct their own training and educational programs. Making students part of these programs shapes unique insights into the latest issues and concerns. These programs provide training that often cannot be found on the university campus and can supplement the educational program of the student.

University Coordination

Whether students become involved off campus through relationships and partnerships involving the business community, or whether their involvement is through a nonprofit organization, educational institution, or government agency, coordination by the university is a key to the success and longevity of community-focused internship and practica programs. Some students will always find employment or volunteer without university involvement. Still, forming and sustaining working relationships with institutions, organizations, and agencies off campus typically requires some minimal support and supervision from the university. Even though informal "handshake" agreements may be appropriate for part-time experiences or activities of short duration, lasting relationships often involve formal, ongoing contracts that define the duties and responsibilities of all parties involved. Carefully crafted agreements between universities and community entities suggest the investment in programs that provides credibility and introduces durability to off-campus student learning experiences.

Conclusion

The role of the metropolitan university is not just to be in the city but to be in partnership with the city (P. Magrath, in Stukel, 1994). Service learning, student teaching, part-time employment, and career opportunities for students build partnerships between university and city. Student involvement plays a major role in the reciprocal commitment of the metropolitan university to its community and the community to its university. Students who have service learning experiences are more likely to engage in social issues and give back to the community. Partnerships allow students to learn to deal with complex social issues, while communities gain attention to their social and economic problems (Ramaley, 1995). The metropolitan university has ample opportunities to serve its students and its communities through partnerships and relationships that reach across campus boundaries. In fact, these arrangements are necessary if the metropolitan university is to effectively serve both students and community. Although a number of these opportunities may be available to many higher education institutions, there is a variety and quantity of possible arrangements unique to the metropolitan university and community.

References

Astin, A. W. "What Matters in College? Four Critical Years Revisited." San Francisco: Jossey-Bass, 1993.

Barnett, M. R., and Phares, D. "The Metropolitan Students." In D. Johnson and D. Bell (eds.), *Metropolitan Universities: An Emerging Model in American Higher Education*. Denton: University of North Texas Press, 1995.

Bok, D. *Beyond the Ivory Tower: Social Responsibilities of the Modern University*. Cambridge, Mass.: Harvard University Press, 1982.

Coles, A. S. "Student Services at Metropolitan Universities." In D. Johnson and D. Bell (eds.), *Metropolitan Universities: An Emerging Model in American Higher Education*. Denton: University of North Texas Press, 1995.

Cooper, J. "Developing Community Partnerships Through Service Learning Programs." *Campus Activities Programming*, 1993, 26 (1), 27–31.

Garman, B. "Civic Education Through Service Learning." ERIC digest. Bloomington, Ind.: ERIC Clearinghouse for Social Studies/Social Science Education, 1995.

Harkavy, I., and Wiewel, W. "University-Community Partnerships: Current State and Future Issues." *Metropolitan Universities: An International Forum*, 1995, *6* (3), 7–14.

Hathaway, C. E., Mulhollan, P. E., and White, K. A. "Metropolitan Universities: Models for the Twenty-First Century." In D. Johnson and D. Bell (eds.), *Metropolitan Universities: An Emerging Model in American Higher Education*. Denton: University of North Texas Press, 1995.

Jacoby, B., and Associates. *Service-Learning in Higher Education: Concepts and Practices*. San Francisco: Jossey-Bass, 1996.

Kuh, G. D., Schuh, J. H., Whitt, E. J., and Associates. *Involving Colleges: Successful Approaches to Fostering Student Learning and Development Outside the Classroom*. San Francisco: Jossey-Bass, 1991.

Lankard, B. A. "Service Learning: Trends and Issues Alerts." ERIC digest. Columbus, OH: ERIC Clearinghouse on Adult, Career, and Vocational Education, 1995.

Lynton, E. "What Is a Metropolitan University?" In D. Johnson and D. Bell (eds.), *Metropolitan Universities: An Emerging Model in American Higher Education*. Denton: University of North Texas Press, 1995.

McWilliams, T. S., and Lewis, B. A. "Another Reconstruction? On Moral Imperatives and Urban Educational Reform." *Metropolitan Universities: An International Forum*, 1994, *5* (2), 43–51.

Ramaley, J. A. "Preparing the Way for Reform in Higher Education: Drawing Upon the Resources of the Community-at-Large." *Metropolitan Universities: An International Forum*, 1995, *6* (3), 29–43.

Smith, R. "School-College Partnerships in Institutional Strategy." Metropolitan Universities: An International Forum, 1994, *5* (2), 33–42.

Stukel, J. J. "Urban and Metropolitan Universities: Leaders of the 21st Century." *Metropolitan Universities: An International Forum*, 1994, *5* (2), 87–92.

Zlotkowski, E. "A New Voice at the Table? Linking Service Learning and the Academy." *Change*, 1996, *28* (1), 20–27.

RICHARD L. PALM *is an assistant professor of higher education in the School of Education, University of Missouri-Kansas City. He was a senior student affairs officer for many years.*

J. DOUGLAS TOMA *is an assistant professor of higher education in the School of Education, University of Missouri-Kansas City.*

Students, faculty, and staff face critically challenging opportunities and pitfalls in support of the urban agenda of metropolitan universities. Institutional leaders must carefully contemplate these issues and leverage the incomparable qualities of city life to the benefit of the university while simultaneously engaging institutional research, instruction, and service activities on behalf of the metropolitan region's needs.

Future Challenges and Priorities

Larry Moneta

In *The University and the City: From Medieval Origins to the Present,* Thomas Bender and colleagues (1988) demonstrate that city and university relationships have been a subject of scholarly and commercial inquiry since at least the twelfth century. With examples drawn from Italy, France, Germany, Great Britain, and the United States, several chapters reveal the complex interrelationships which have characterized "town-gown" interactions for the eight-hundred-year span covered by that text (Adamany, 1994; Johnson and Bell, 1995). Further, the work suggests that despite nearly a millennium of evolutionary growth and expansions, contemporary urban-located universities face similar issues and challenges as those once confronted by Bologna, Cambridge, and Heidelberg.

These challenges center around the primary connecting points between the university and its host city: economic, cultural, social, educational, and political elements. These elements are substantially influenced by the geographical distinctions of the city, the location of the university within the city (and the nature of the adjacent communities), the historical roots and mission of the institution, and the nature of its student body, faculty, and staff. These are but a small sample of the great number of transactions and interactions between the city and its metropolitan universities.

A "concentric circle" approach, with the university in the center (for the sake of this discussion), offers a useful framework for review of these concerns and discussion of future challenges and suggestions.

The Metropolitan University

Several distinctions emerge when considering the nature of the formal campus property. The university consists of a collection of people: its students, faculty, and staff, engaged in a widely diverse set of functions including teaching,

NEW DIRECTIONS FOR STUDENT SERVICES, no. 79, Fall 1997 © Jossey-Bass Publishers researching, managing, and laboring, within a variety of facilities. Each of these elements offers specific challenges in light of metropolitan interdependencies.

Students. Metropolitan universities often recruit more heavily from the local communities than from outside their own metropolitan sphere. Even institutions of national and international renown, however, are likely to have expectations of enhanced access for local citizens (Richardson and Bender, 1985). These expectations may range from the formal (as, for example, in the case of the Philadelphia Mayor's Scholarship program at the University of Pennsylvania) to the informal, where institutions are "expected" to admit a significant number of students from the local communities.

Recruitment intentions range from exclusively local to international; they define the preferred student profile for metropolitan universities. Despite these intentions, however, most institutions can expect increased pressure to admit and serve even larger percentages of students from adjacent communities. Assuming a need for significant financial aid for these students and their families, the immediate economic consequences of response to these demands may be substantial. Metropolitan institutions are hard pressed to accommodate this need, and public institutions will appeal to local and state sources for increased allocations. Private institutions face continued challenges to their tuition rates in order to provide adequate support. This may negatively impact their aid discount and the resources available to support the academic mission.

Similarly, metropolitan universities face enormous pressure to admit marginally acceptable students who increasingly turn to the university to compensate for the declining quality of urban, public elementary and secondary education. Open admission metropolitan universities can expect greater demand for remedial educational opportunities, academic counseling, and course variety. Selective institutions face criticism for holding steadfast to standards that effectively deny access to graduates of most surrounding high schools (Kuh and Vesper, 1991).

As demonstrated in earlier chapters, race and age characteristics have a dramatic impact on metropolitan universities. Increasingly, cities populate their metropolitan institutions with older students and students of varying race and ethnicity. Many work full-time while attending classes, and many are raising children of their own, with and without partners. Preferred campus activities and institutional services differ, then, for some (but not all) metropolitan clients. Metropolitan universities face the daunting task of serving traditional students with on-campus housing and residence life programs, student government and activities, intramural and intercollegiate athletics, and the like while simultaneously attending to the needs of nontraditional students who seek child care, commuter access, academic support, and immediate problem solving (Borden and Gentemann, 1993; Elliot, 1994).

The diversification of metropolitan universities also suggests that such institutions continue to face growing tensions between various populations. However, it is likely that opportunities and solutions to address the real and perceived balkanization of our colleges and universities are found at metropolitan universities. It is these institutions that have the critical mass of diverse constituents and that are forced to develop multicultural programs and services resulting in genuine pluralistic communities.

Rural and suburban students who choose to attend metropolitan institutions have unique exposure to urban life. Their experiences are both positive and negative. Metropolitan institutions are confronted by their obligation to protect and sometimes insulate these students from the threats of urban plights. However, they have equal responsibility and a unique opportunity to enable these students to understand the needs of American cities. Student activities and orientation efforts at these institutions must include opportunities for students to engage with the city: visits to museums; shopping excursions; and citywide recreational, social, and cultural activities should be part of the extracurricular experience.

Metropolitan universities face unprecedented pressure to admit, serve, and graduate local students. They are also expected to educate uninformed rural and suburban students about the riches and needs of the cities. These pressures strain admissions standards, financial aid formulas, service and support models, and career preparation resources. They also stimulate creative thinking about contemporary problems, including race relations, family support models, and personal empowerment.

Faculty. At many colleges and universities throughout the nation, critical commentary can be found about the excessive specialization (and subspecialization) of the faculty. Faculty members frequently are accused of having greater commitment to their discipline than to their home institutions. In addition, many decry the absence of high-quality instruction at institutions that emphasize research as a primary expectation of the faculty (and that recruit faculty members who prefer to engage in research as their primary activity).

Service, that often forgotten third enterprise, is more readily portrayed as a valued faculty expectation than it is demonstrated in action. However, for metropolitan universities service may become a fundamentally distinguishing academic characteristic as well as an essential expectation. Through service and, in particular, service learning, metropolitan universities can best integrate teaching and research on behalf of higher education's primary agenda: the development and exchange of knowledge.

Metropolitan universities have unparalleled opportunity to reform faculty roles and disciplinary limitations by focusing on their urban agendas. Illustrations abound throughout the country. Wayne State University features nursing training that addresses the needs of the homeless, and legal training with an emphasis on domestic violence (Greiner, 1994). Most metropolitan universities can undoubtedly list a fair number of similar initiatives suggesting attention to local concerns. However, few have significantly reconstructed the overall curriculum in ways that emphasize the urban landscape as the foundation for research, teaching, and public service.

Evidence of such a shift in curricular construct and academic focus is found when academic disciplines and institutional departments are supplemented in increasing numbers with interdisciplinary institutes, centers, and majors. Business, sociology, and psychology faculty can collaborate on studies of urban small-business development; medicine, nursing, sociology, and education have much to share on the health needs and health education of urban families; engineering, physics, and business faculty have collective expertise on urban utilities distribution systems. Opportunities (and needs) for cooperative and collaborative interdisciplinary investigations and developments abound in every area of urban activity.

Faculty generally demonstrate an inclination to engage in productive inquiry and instruction—even those faculty involved in the most esoteric research. Current reward systems, particularly at research institutions, discourage faculty from pursuing projects like those just described. The most respected refereed journals remain steadfast in their disciplinary foundations, and many institutions reward tenure predominantly according to faculty success in getting published in those journals. The growth of interdisciplinary (and urban-grounded) inquiry requires that metropolitan universities change the rules. Faculty merit salary determinations, and perhaps, tenure decisions need to take into account faculty academic activities emphasizing discovery of knowledge and development of initiatives that inform and improve the status of their home cities.

Staff. Several issues and challenges related to staff and employees of metropolitan universities are worth comment. For professional staff, one such issue is competency. Although many skills—such as managing residence halls and student unions, offering career and personal counseling, advising student clubs and organizations, and running sports and recreation programs—may be interchangeable with institutions of all types and sizes, metropolitan universities require that their staff translate many of these services and activities to the diverse populations in attendance at these institutions. Development of competency requirements for staff at such institutions is critical. It is incumbent upon individual metropolitan universities and consortia of institutions to develop performance standards and standards of base-line knowledge that are essential for those who choose to join metropolitan universities as staff.

Concurrently, these institutions are challenged to develop training programs that can transform the best practitioners from all institutions into successful practitioners at metropolitan institutions. Human resource departments must redefine their roles to include opportunities for acculturation to the urban mission and goals of the metropolitan university and to successful practices relevant to these circumstances. Student affairs staff must engage in staff development activities that enhance their appreciation and understanding of the urban agenda and the implications for student services and student development.

Clerical and service employees at metropolitan universities frequently reside in the cities and their immediate environs. These staff, so critical to the daily functioning of the institution, often reflect the racial and ethnic composition of the city's residential base and thus are disproportionately of color, single parents, and limited income. They are also highly sensitive to the needs of their communities and well versed in the reputation of their employer as either

Economic Influences. In many cities, the local metropolitan university serves as one of the largest employers. The payroll and, especially, payroll taxes provided by the university serve as a major economic engine for the city and the region. Through various direct services, these institutions allow cities to avoid an assortment of expenses. For example, Wayne State University provides $30 million of medical care to the Detroit community through its medical school and hospital. Further, although they only constitute 20 percent of the nation's acute care beds, academic medical centers provide half of the total charity medical care (Cisneros, 1995).

Metropolitan universities also are major spenders and annually allot enormous amounts of money for goods and services required by the institution. Add the money spent by students, their families, faculty, staff, alumni, visitors, and local businesses on behalf of the university, and one can see the tremendous impact the metropolitan university has on the economic status of the city and the region.

The institution's choices of preferred vendors can be a substantial economic influence in the metropolitan region. Many institutions have established buying programs that favor local service and product providers. The University of Pennsylvania sponsors a west Philadelphia purchasing program that directs acquisitions of office supplies and various services to local vendors. In many cases, these programs are linked to multicultural support commitments and enable small, minority-owned businesses to access the vast expenditure pools offered by universities.

University billing and payment practices can affect the metropolitan economy. By extending credit to small, local businesses, the university can support the emergence of local industries and commercial and retail establishments. These kinds of businesses are also extremely susceptible to cash-flow problems, and expeditious payment of invoices can have a profound effect on the success of the enterprises.

By utilizing strategic investment of (sometimes immense) endowments, metropolitan universities exert another valuable economic stimulus upon the local environment. Investments in local bond efforts; development of assorted mortgage support programs for faculty, staff, and perhaps students (most likely graduate or professional); and purchase of securities and stocks offered by local corporate partners all contribute to the health and growth of the regional economy.

The recent movement in higher education toward consideration of outsourcing and privatization of various university services has a substantial impact on the local economy. In many cases, privatization enables institutions to reduce positions. This directly impacts local tax revenues, but when the use of a private manager or operator results in a significant loss of collectively bargained positions, the local economy may suffer much greater losses both financially and in labor relations with other bargaining units. Negative relationships with local unions are likely to have serious impact on metropolitan universities, where one is more likely to find strong union presence.

However, when use of an outsourcing partner is in the best interest of the metropolitan university, strategic selection of such partners may serve to enhance both the institution's and the region's interests. This can be accomplished by selecting local providers or by establishing contract provisions that favor employment of local citizenry without violating public bidding requirements. Private operators can also be encouraged or contractually bound to utilize similar billing, purchasing, and investment strategies as outlined above.

Many decry the preferred tax status of higher education institutions, which liberates them from tax liabilities. However, metropolitan universities that recognize the privileges associated with tax avoidance have often agreed to provide payment in lieu of taxes: subsidy or repayment for fire response services, licensing and inspection activities, and other city-provided or mandated activities generally supported by the local tax base.

When all direct economic stimuli have been examined and implemented, metropolitan universities can also turn to indirect contributors. One example might be the use of "loaned experts" such as senior administrators or distinguished faculty who might offer guidance in exchange for course relief. These people can be deployed to assist local governance efforts, small-business development, regional planning, environmental support, and the like.

Educational Influences. That universities, metropolitan or otherwise, wield significant educational influence should come as no particular revelation. However, metropolitan universities have distinct opportunities to offer educational services to the local marketplace and communities. Delivery of degree programs, continuing education, noncredit curricula, and formal training services is exceptionally valuable to the quality of life of city and regional residents.

Obviously, the primary educational contribution that can be made by the metropolitan university is access to degree-granting programs. Full-time and part-time studies uniquely tailored to support the diversity of inhabitants in city communities can be most effective in serving the population. These distinctions might include late (or early) day or evening courses to enable students to hold full-time day jobs. Weekend, extended-session courses have been used effectively for students who cannot attend weekday class meetings. Supportive institutions also offer access to on-campus child care, transportation support, and other creative logistical initiatives that could lower barriers for access to coursework. One innovative institution even offers classes on the commuter trains traveling into the city. Metropolitan universities will be challenged to consider further such inventive solutions to enabling student access to classes and academic support.

Of greatest use in supporting remote educational access is the notion of technology-enhanced distance learning. Cities may be best suited to exploit distance learning opportunities given the plethora of cable television and computer networking options in place. Many universities have invested heavily in teleconferencing and videotaping infrastructures that might be deployed in concert with local cable providers to bring televised coursework to homebound students. The advent of the Internet and, especially, the World Wide Web has created myriad opportunities for remote delivery of educational services and curricula, opportunities that should be explored and exploited.

Educational support for school-age children is particularly suited to metropolitan universities. City schools are desperate for support, and universities can fill that need by providing tutors, mentors, and aides for pupils and by offering advanced-degree study opportunities for teachers and school administrators. Those universities with museums, performing arts facilities, and other cultural attractions are particularly well positioned to support school educational efforts by offering affordable access to these facilities and by supporting them with faculty, students, and staff who can lead follow-up discussions and analysis.

Continuing educational efforts have become extremely attractive both for formal certification requirements (as for accountants, realtors, and other professionals) and for personal enlightenment. Metropolitan universities can add to the richness of city life by offering nondegree (and noncredit) seminars and courses on a wide variety of topics. These sessions are both informative and often entertaining and serve as a good source of revenue to the institution. Many institutions have been quite successful in developing "elderhostel" programs, which support the continuing educational efforts of senior citizens. With the graying of the baby boomers at hand, this is clearly a growth industry!

Cultural Influences. Metropolitan universities offer tremendous opportunities for cultural interaction with the local community. Those fortunate enough to have museums or galleries affiliated with their institutions can provide access to the community-at-large. Some institutions formalize these opportunities through such community outreach efforts as inviting schools to visit, offering instructional programs, and enabling the community to use these spaces for receptions and other appropriate gatherings.

Cultural contributions can also be made by those universities not maintaining formal museums. In many cases, academic departments own various collections of great interest to the urban public. Libraries may have rare book collections; music and art departments feature student and faculty created productions; student performing arts groups offer various drama, vocal, and related productions; English departments feature poetry readings and other forms of creative expression; and political science faculty invite world leaders to campus to give visiting lectures or public addresses.

Undoubtedly, this list can be substantially extended with a modicum of campus activity scanning. The fundamental challenge to metropolitan universities is to open access to these wonderful opportunities. Such access is mutually supportive to the community and the institution. The community benefits from the cultural contribution offered by the university, and the university benefits from the positive public appreciation, from the possibility that the neighborhoods surrounding the campus may become desirable for residence, and in same cases from user fees.

The university has often been noted as a cultural mecca and center of arts and creative expression. The metropolitan university's commitment to sharing these opportunities is highly desired and appreciated. Community appreciation is often a precursor to the next area of concern: the political.

Political Influences. By virtue of all the issues and opportunities noted above, and through extensive lobbying and governmental relations efforts, universities have developed significant clout in political circles. This is especially important to metropolitan universities in need of fostering positive relationships with their local elected officials. The typically large number of students who populate metropolitan universities offers a voter bloc, and student lobbying efforts can be quite effective in advancing preferred causes and movements.

Institutions can empower students to be active in political causes and campaigns by sponsoring or supporting voter registration drives and inviting community activists and elected officials to the campus. Student commitment to urban policies and social issues can be substantially influenced by the metropolitan university's attention (directed or benign) to community activism and the political processes for effecting change. However, an institutional decision to enable student participation in the political process should be well considered: once ignited, it may spread widely and beyond the scope of the institution's original interests.

Institutional political influence is also advanced within the local community by partnerships between campus and community officials. University fire safety personnel can work in concert with their municipal counterparts to develop appropriate safety standards and codes. Similarly, city building codes and licensing requirements can be influenced by university staff empowered by the extensive real estate holdings and expertise existing among campus employees. Used wisely, such influence can result in improved standards and laws. Used capriciously, metropolitan universities can find themselves resented by the local public, and more importantly by local elected bodies. An angry city council can be a powerful enemy with the power to block necessary zoning changes for the next new campus building. A friendly city council is much preferred.

Conclusion

Metropolitan universities are incredibly well positioned to be major forces on behalf of their cities and metropolitan regions. They have the resources, talent, and opportunities to be of tremendous service to these areas not just through traditional forms of community service but also by the power of their expenditures, the stimulus of their cultural holdings, the authority in their "voices," and the strength of their convictions. It is critical, given the stresses and diminishing resources available to city agencies, governing bodies, and the populace at large, that metropolitan universities exploit all these opportunities for their communities (Stukel, 1994).

Student affairs professionals are particularly well suited to address these challenges through the services featured and the close contact held with students. Residence hall staff have the capacity to house local summer camps, urban elderhostels, or even homeless shelters. Student activities staffs have the opportunity to feature individual and group volunteer efforts or leadership training programs that include modules on metropolitan issues. Health services units can offer community immunization programs, extend peer health education into the local schools, and offer anonymous HIV testing to the local community.

The student affairs profession has a proud history of service to our students, our institutions, and our communities. Inherent in the prime directives of the field are commitments to human development and societal enhancement. As such, student affairs staff at metropolitan universities have the privilege and the responsibility to extend traditional programmatic, service, and educational practices to support of the urban initiatives identified above. Student affairs staff, then, become exemplary role models for the full spectrum of activities that make up the modern metropolitan university.

References

Adamany, D. "Sustaining University Values While Reinventing University Commitments to Our Cities." *Teachers College Record,* 1994, *95* (3), 324–331.

Bender, T. *The University and the City: From Medieval Origins to the Present.* New York: Oxford University Press, 1988.

Borden, V.M.H., and Gentemann, K. *Campus Community and Student Priorities at a Metropolitan University.* Paper presented at the annual forum of the Association for Institutional Research, Chicago, 1993. (ED 360 920)

Cisneros, H. G. *The University and the Urban Challenge.* Washington D.C.: Department of Housing and Urban Development, 1995. (ED 388 155)

Elliot, P. G. *The Urban Campus: Educating the New Majority for the New Century.* Phoenix: Oryx Press, 1994.

Greiner, W. R. "'In the Total of All These Acts': How Can American Universities Address the Urban Agenda?" *Teachers College Record,* 1994, *95* (3), 317–323.

Grobman, A. B. *Urban State Universities: An Unfinished National Agenda.* Westport, Conn.: Praeger, 1988.

Johnson, D. M., and Bell, D. A. (eds). *Metropolitan Universities: An Emerging Model in American Higher Education.* Denton: University of North Texas Press, 1995.

Kuh, G. D., and Vesper, N. *Influences on Student Learning at Metropolitan Institutions.* Paper presented at the annual meeting of the Association for the Study of Higher Education, Boston, 1991. (ED 339 316)

Richardson, R. C., and Bender, L. W. *Students in Urban Settings: Achieving the Baccalaureate Degree.* ASHE-ERIC Higher Education Report no. 6, 1985.

Stukel, J. J. "Urban and Metropolitan Universities: Leaders of the 21st Century." *Metropolitan Universities,* 1994, *5* (2), 87–92.

LARRY MONETA is associate vice provost for university life at the University of Pennsylvania and adjunct professor in the Higher Education Division of the Graduate School of Education at the university. He is presently serving on the NASPA national board of directors.

Selected Resources on Serving Students at Metropolitan Universities

Marcia Stevens, Jennifer M. Calhoun

This chapter contains information about resources for those interested in further research and discussion about serving students at metropolitan universities.

Books and Monographs

Bender, T. (ed.). *The University and the City: From Medieval Origins to the Present.* New York: Oxford University Press, 1988.
This collection of essays helps define the history and relationship between the university and the city by focusing on medieval origins, early modern revitalization, the metropolitan university, and the modern university and the modern city. The essays examine the university's connection to society and the influence of local culture and politics.

Elliot, P. G. *The Urban Campus: Educating the New Majority for the New Century.* Phoenix: Oryx Press, 1994.
This book addresses the development and growth of urban campuses; the role of urban institutions; the nature of urban students; issues related to urban faculty; new educational demands placed on urban institutions; partnerships between urban institutions and community, public schools, and business and industry; and ways urban campus can fulfill their roles and meet the challenges of the future.

Grobman, A. B. *Urban State Universities: An Unfinished National Agenda*. Westport, Conn.: Praeger, 1988.

The author uses data from a 1986–87 survey of thirty-six selected state institutions to contrast urban and nonurban state universities on students, academic programs and access, faculty and staff, student services and facilities, and community partnerships. He offers ten suggestions in the areas of academic programs, residential facilities, urban grant university legislation, faculty reward system, school-university cooperation, remedial instruction, consortia, state allocations, alumni support, and the role of the president.

Harrington, T. F. *Student Personnel Work in Urban Colleges*. New York: Intex Educational Publishers, 1974.

This book primarily addresses college student personnel work in general but includes material specific to urban higher education.

Johnson, D. M., and Bell, D. A. (eds.). *Metropolitan Universities: An Emerging Model in American Higher Education*. Denton: University of North Texas Press, 1995.

The editors selected twenty-nine articles from the journal *Metropolitan Universities: An International Forum* for this anthology. The articles focus on the unique mission and characteristics of metropolitan universities and the special challenges they face. Topics include philosophy, history, and mission; student affairs; faculty roles and responsibilities; partnerships in the education community; community-university relationships; continuing and distance education; professional education and the arts; leadership needs and issues; and the future of metropolitan universities.

Jones, J. D., and Damron, J. *Student Affairs Programs at Universities in Urban Settings*. Washington, D.C.: National Association of State Universities and Land Grant Colleges, 1987.

This monograph identifies the characteristics of urban institutions and the student populations served; addresses the priorities placed on services, programs, activities, and facilities provided; and proposes strategies to strengthen student affairs services at these institutions. The authors examine the diverse missions and purposes of urban institutions, collaboration with academic units, retention efforts, and articulation policies with junior and community colleges that feed into urban institutions. Emphasis is also placed on how student affairs professionals are meeting the demands and expectations of their urban students.

Journals

Metropolitan Universities: An International Forum; published quarterly; individual subscription: $30/one year, $55/two years, $75/three years; institution subscription: $68/one year, $120/two years, $156/three years (Towson State University, 7800 York Rd., Towson, MD 21204–7097; telephone: (410) 830–3468; fax (404) 830–3456).

Organizations

The *AASCU/NASULGC Office of Urban and Metropolitan Programs* represents a joint commitment by the American Association of State Colleges and Universities and the National Association of State Universities and Land-Grant Colleges to promote the effectiveness of member institutions in the ongoing national effort to increase cooperation between universities and urban communities. The Office of Urban and Metropolitan Programs develops policy and action agendas in cooperation with the leadership of the AASCU Commission on the Urban Metropolitan Agenda and the NASULGC Commission on the Urban Agenda. The office also maintains a Clearinghouse on Urban and Community Service based on the 1994 Survey of Urban and Metropolitan Universities, which was updated in 1996.

For more information, contact:

AASCU/NASULGC Office of Urban and Metropolitan Programs
One Dupont Circle, Suite 700
Washington, DC 20036-1192
Telephone: (202) 293-7070
Fax: (202) 296-5819
Web site: http://www.aascu.nche.edu/services/aip/urban/overview.htm

The *Coalition of Urban and Metropolitan Universities* brings together universities that share the mission of striving for national excellence while contributing to the economic development, social health, and cultural vitality of the urban or metropolitan centers that they serve. The coalition sponsors an annual conference, the *Metropolitan Universities Journal: An International Forum,* and additional publications.

For more information, contact:

The Coalition of Urban and Metropolitan Universities
Dr. Bill McKee
University of North Texas
P.O. Box 13737
Denton, TX 76203
Telephone: (817) 565-2477
Fax: (817) 565-4998
Web site: http://www.ucf.edu/metropolitan/coalition.html

The *Urban Colleges and Universities Network,* sponsored by the National Association of Student Personnel Administrators, provides a forum for continued growth and development through programming and mutual exchange of information. The network offers conference programs, an Internet listserv, networking opportunities, and newsletters.

For more information, contact:

National Association of Student Personnel Administrators
Drawer No. 0023
Washington, DC 20073-0023
Fax: (202) 797-1157
Web site: http://naspa.com

Data Exchange

The *Public Urban University Student Affairs Data Exchange* is a coordinated sub-scription survey sponsored by the chief student affairs offices of fifteen large public urban universities (enrollment over ten thousand). The annual survey covers student affairs cost centers, enrollment, finance, graduation and reten-tion rates, degrees awarded, degree enrollment, student aid, standard scores, and ad hoc information. Urban university CSAOs meet twice a year, and data managers once yearly, to review the annual report and plan new ad hoc surveys. Membership is open to student affairs officers of large public urban universities.

For more information, contact:

Dr. Caryl K. Smith
University of Akron
Akron, OH 44325-4701
Telephone: (216) 972-7907
Fax: (216) 972-8842
Web site: http://www.edmin.com/jma/puburba1.html

Internet Resources

Subscribe to these lists by sending a one-line message to the listserv address noted. The one-line message must read:

subscribe <name of list> <your first name> <your last name>

You will receive a message that confirms you have been successfully joined to the list and provides additional information.

The NASPA Urban Colleges and Universities Network Listserv
Listserv name: Urban-coll
Listserv address: networks@listserv.naspa.org

The AASCU/NASULGC Office of Urban and Metropolitan Programs Listserv
Listserv name: Urb/metro Alert
Listserv address: urbmetro@aascu.nche.edu

MARCIA STEVENS is assistant dean of students at Wichita State University.

JENNIFER M. CALHOUN is completing her bachelor's degree at Wichita State Univer-sity, where she serves as an intern in the Division of Student Affairs.

INDEX

83

ORDERING INFORMATION

NEW DIRECTIONS FOR STUDENT SERVICES is a series of paperback books that offers guidelines and programs for aiding students in their total development—emotional, social, and physical, as well as intellectual. Books in the series are published quarterly in Spring, Summer, Fall, and Winter and are available for purchase by subscription as well as individually.

SUBSCRIPTIONS cost $54.00 for individuals (a savings of 35 percent over single-copy prices) and $90.00 for institutions, agencies, and libraries. Standing orders are accepted. New York residents, add local sales tax for subscriptions. (For subscriptions outside the United States, add $7.00 for shipping via surface mail or $25.00 for air mail. Orders *must be prepaid* in U.S. dollars by check drawn on a U.S. bank or charged to VISA, MasterCard, or American Express.)

SINGLE COPIES cost $22.00 plus shipping (see below) when payment accompanies order. California, New Jersey, New York, and Washington, D.C., residents, please include appropriate sales tax. Canadian residents, add GST and any local taxes. Billed orders will be charged shipping and handling. No billed shipments to post office boxes. (Orders from outside the United States *must be prepaid* by check drawn on a U.S. bank or charged to VISA, MasterCard, or American Express.)

SHIPPING (SINGLE COPIES ONLY): $30.00 and under, add $5.50; to $50.00, add $6.50; to $75.00, add $7.50; to $100.00, add $9.00; to $150.00, add $10.00.

ALL PRICES are subject to change.

DISCOUNTS FOR QUANTITY ORDERS are available. Please write to the address below for information.

ALL ORDERS must include either the name of an individual or an official purchase order number. Please submit your order as follows:
   Subscriptions: specify series and year subscription is to begin
   Single copies: include individual title code (such as SS55)

MAIL ALL ORDERS TO:
   Jossey-Bass Publishers
   350 Sansome Street
   San Francisco, California 94104-1342

PHONE subscription or single-copy orders toll-free at (888) 378-2537 or at (415) 433-1767 (toll call).

FAX orders toll-free to: (800) 605-2665

FOR SUBSCRIPTION SALES OUTSIDE OF THE UNITED STATES, contact any international subscription agency or Jossey-Bass directly.